AF477684

GUDRUN KEMSA

NEW YORK, NEW YORK

KERBER PHOTO

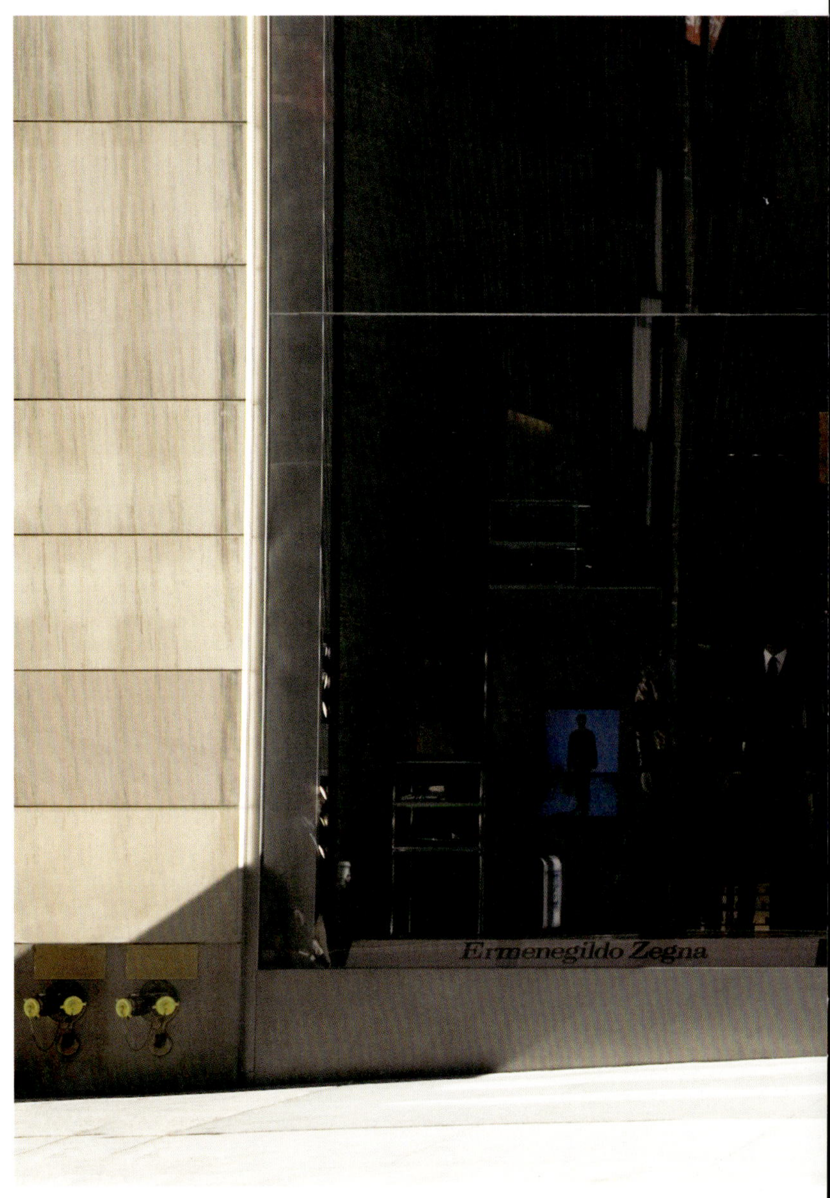

5th Avenue 3, 2009

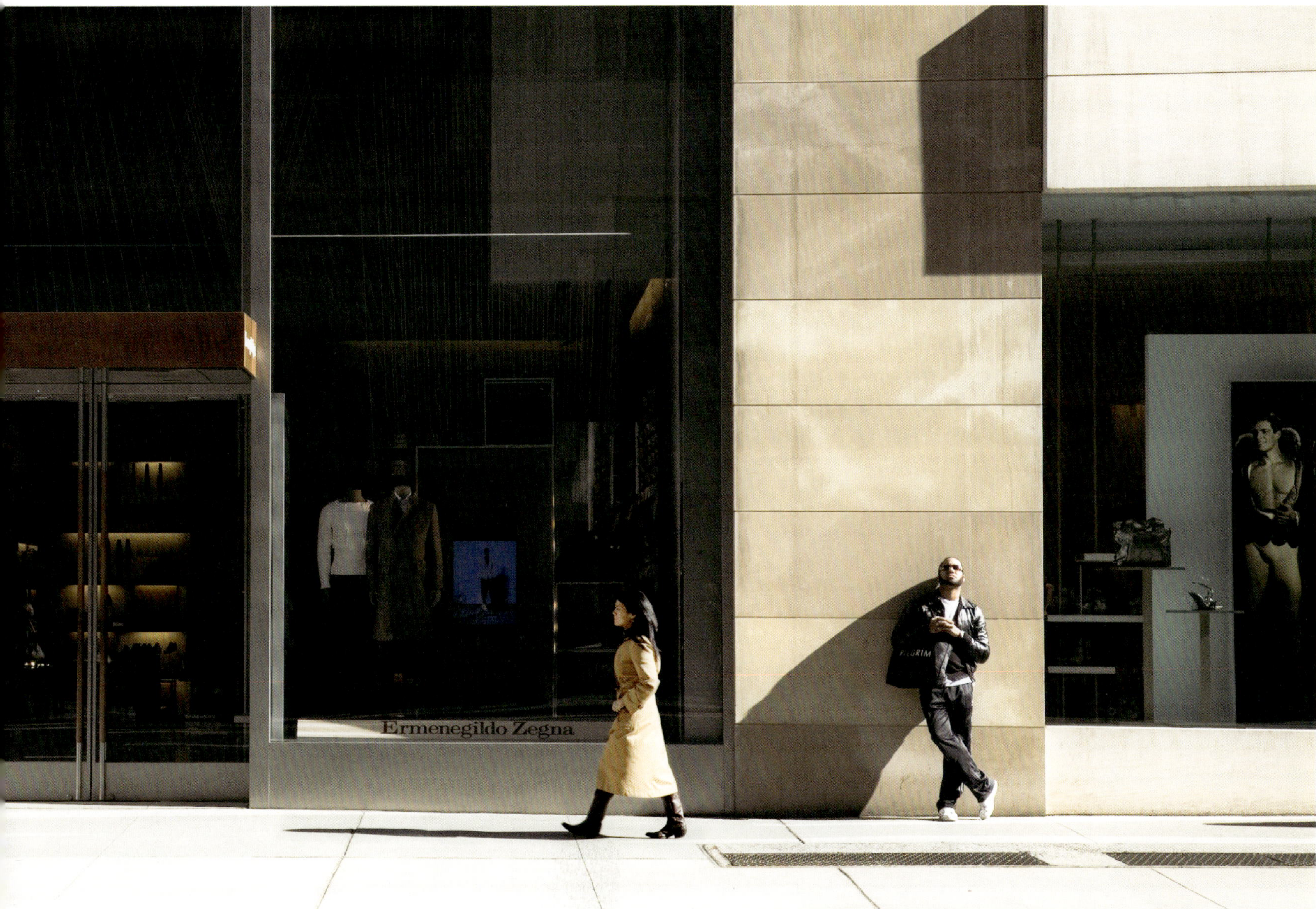

Ermenegildo Zegna

„Mein Motiv ist das Gegenüber"
Anmerkungen zu Gudrun Kemsas New York-Bildern
von Tayfun Belgin

In einem kurzen Beitrag zur Bilderserie *Manhattan* äußert sich die Künstlerin so:

Die urbane Architektur wird zu einer Bühne, auf der die Personen agieren. Das Licht ist hell und klar, und fast wirkt es, als ob es nur dafür geschaffen wurde, die ganze Szenerie dieser riesigen Bühne auf natürliche Weise perfekt auszuleuchten …

Die Welt ist eine Bühne, vor allem in den Städten finden Tag für Tag unendliche Aufführungen statt, in denen sich Menschen gezwungen oder leger und frei bewegen. Realität ereignet sich im Plural, niemals erhalten wir nur ein einziges Bild dieser Welt. Alles ist im Fluss, wie die Vorsokratiker uns lehrten. Alles fließt, und nichts bleibt; es gibt nur ein ewiges Werden und Wandeln. Zeit und Bewegung werden daher zu unseren Konstanten. Die Bilder veranschaulichen auf ihre Weise, was wir unter Bewegung und Vergänglichkeit begrifflich fassen. Jenseits von Zufälligkeit mag es ein konzeptueller Impuls für Gudrun Kemsa gewesen sein, als sie sich entschied, mit ihrer Fotografie bewegte Bilder zu generieren. Immer wieder begegnen uns in den Fotografien Menschen, die in Bewegung sind, die schnell oder langsam gehen, sich umdrehen, verharren, anderen begegnen und irgendwann vor einer Ampel ihr Gehen einstellen, um sich kurze Zeit später wieder zu bewegen.

Gudrun Kemsa beobachtet. Sie hat ein Gegenüber. Das ist ihr Motiv. Sie ist die eine Seite, das Gegenüber ist die andere. Sie beobachtet, während andere agieren: eine eigentümliche Asymmetrie, würde Niklas Luhmann sagen. Stiller Beobachter und bewegte Partner, wobei Letztere eher unfreiwillig zu Agierenden dieser Bilder werden. Gudrun Kemsa war mehrmals in New York, und zwar zu sehr unterschiedlichen Zeiten. Dass gerade Midtown nahezu alle Besucher der Stadt begeistert, liegt auf der Hand. Wir befinden uns im Zentrum des Hochkapitalismus. Dieser Teil New Yorks generiert Bilder von bisweilen unendlicher Schönheit auf den Straßen und Plätzen. Ein anderer Teil dieser nie ruhenden Insel offenbart eine gänzlich andere, sehr eigentümliche Ästhetik: Downtown, Little Italy oder Harlem – auch diese Stadtteile werden oft fotografiert und sind in unzähligen Filmen präsent. Doch sie inspirieren zu Erzählungen, die nicht im Fokus von Gudrun Kemsa liegen. In diesen Regionen entstehen Mythen von Helden, von Mafiabossen genauso wie von genialen Jazz-Musikern. Diese Erzählungen bieten Stoff für Filme jeglicher Art, von Liebesfilmen bis hin zu brutalen Gangsterfilmen. New York bietet den besten Ort der USA für Überhöhungen und Neurosen, von der Wall Street bis zu den bevorzugten Drehorten Woody Allens.

Gudrun Kemsas beobachtendes Auge nimmt Aktionen wahr, die uns mangels Zeit oder Interesse entgleiten. Wir sehen ihre Motive nicht, richtiger formuliert: Wir nehmen dieses Geschehen auf der Straße nicht mit ihren Augen wahr. Um teilzunehmen an dieser fluiden Welt, die keinerlei Substanz hervorbringt, benötigt man Zeit. Wenn Zeit gegeben ist, gewinnt das Spiel mit der flüchtigen Welt der Straße an Faszination. Zeit ist die Bedingung für Gudrun Kemsas Fotografie. Wir als Betrachter gehen in aller Regel vorbei an den Inszenierungen, die die Fotografin herbeiführt. Sie aber beherrscht das Prinzip des Zueinander und Miteinander. Gudrun Kemsa beobachtet konzentriert die gegenüberliegende Straßenseite und wartet so lange, bis Menschen, die sie nicht kennt, zueinander finden und ihr ein Bildmotiv liefern. In diesem Moment werden sie durch eine kurze Berührung des Auslösers verewigt. Konkret: In dem Bild *42nd Street 3, 2018* treffen vor einem Prada-Geschäft zwei Menschen auf dem Bürgersteig aufeinander, die sich vielleicht zuvor noch nie begegnet sind. Am linken Rand des Schaufensters schaut ein Mann nach rechts in Richtung einer elegant gekleideten Dame, die auf ihn zuschreitet. Es ist dieser entscheidende Moment, um mit Cartier-Bresson zu sprechen, der Gudrun Kemsa dazu bewegte, diese zwei für sie anonymen Personen aufzunehmen. Beide Personen – der Tourist mit Kappe und 3/4-Hose links, wie auch die New Yorkerin in einem grünen Kleid, die mit ihrem Handy telefoniert – sind im Moment des Fotografiert-Werdens Akteure vor einer gewaltigen Betonarchitektur. Sie betonen die vertikale Dimension des Gebäudes. Während die telefonierende Dame das Prada-Geschäft schon fast erreicht hat, steht eine weitere Dame rechts noch im Rahmen des Eingangsbereichs des Hauses Nr. 724 hinter ihr. Ein Mann steht an der linken vertikalen Kante des Ladenlokals. Das Geschäft selbst mit seinen Auslagen an Kleiderpuppen ist in diese helle Betonarchitektur gleichsam eingelassen. Hier offenbart sich ein Prinzip der aktuellen Fotografie von Gudrun Kemsa: Sie komponiert ihre Fotografien mit Basislinien, mit der Vertikalen und Horizontalen. Hinzu kommen Fenster als Rahmen für Passanten, Türeingänge mit strenger Geometrie, die als Leitachsen dienen: Ampeln, Säulen, Bushaltestellen mit einer Informations-Steele, herunterhängende Lampen an Gebäuden usw.

Ein differenzierter Blick gilt jenen Fotografien, die nicht mehr das „flache" Gegenüber einer Architektur als Grundmotiv haben, sondern eine Ecksituation zeigen. Zum einen bietet sich hier eine andere Tiefe an, zum anderen erweitert sich der Rahmen der Handlung. Menschen gehen von links nach rechts und umgekehrt; sie überqueren die Straße an einer Ampel, einige verharren für kurze Zeit. Das hinter ihnen liegende große Ladenlokal hat nicht mehr ganz so viel Präsenz. An dieser Stelle lässt sich fragen, ob dieser Art der Street-Fotografie eine Erzählstruktur inhärent ist. Festzustellen ist, dass wir in diesen Bildern eine Darstellung haben, die ein Geschehen wiedergibt. Es handelt sich allerdings nicht um eine klassische Narration, es gibt keinen Akteur, der etwas erzählt. Hier begegnen sich Menschen auf der Straße, auf einer Treppe in der Metro, die sich nicht kennen und über die bildlich in einem bestimmten Moment berichtet wird. In der Bilderfolge *Subway* von 2018 werden die Zufälligkeiten noch stärker herausgestellt. Hier, im Untergrund der Stadt, scheint die Anonymität noch stärker zu sein als auf der Straße.

Bezüglich der drei klassischen Einheiten Zeit, Raum und Handlung, die Aristoteles bei einem Drama als notwendig erachtete, haben wir in den Bildern von Gudrun Kemsa eine Übereinstimmung. Die Fotografierten befinden sich zu einer bestimmten Zeit am selben Ort und handeln. Allerdings lässt sich in diesen Fotografien kein Drama in fünf Akten nachvollziehen, eher ist das Ephemere der Grundtenor. Insofern ist vom Begriff der Erzählung im klassischen Sinne abzusehen, eher haben wir es hier mit einer unverbindlichen Erzählung zu tun. Das Foto bringt Menschen zusammen, die in diesem Moment Teil einer Erzählung sein könnten. Im auslösenden Moment ist jeder Figur eine bestimmte Rolle zugeeignet. Es gibt stehende Menschen, schreitende, wartende, lesende etc. Alle sind auf einem Bild, jedoch wird nicht über sie alle erzählt, sie sind lediglich dargestellt.

Alle Dargestellten nehmen Teil an einer Welt, die sich dem äußeren Schein widmet. Hierzu gehören einerseits die fantastischen Geschäfte auf der Renommiermeile Fifth Avenue wie auch die grandiose Architektur, die wir auch in Paris (La Défense), in Berlin, London oder Dubai wiederfinden. Zu allen Orten begab sich Gudrun Kemsa und fand sich atmosphärisch ein. An keinem der Orte, schon gar nicht in Venice Beach oder Al Merraija (Dubai), nahm Gudrun Kemsa eine Situation bei regnerischem Wetter auf. Regen gehört nicht zum Konzept dieser Fotografie. Bei Regen agieren die Menschen bisweilen hektisch und sind – vor allem in Industrienationen – eher ungehalten. Die Souveränität der Bewegung ist eingeschränkt; jene Freiheit, die Gudrun Kemsa bei ihren Akteuren einfängt, ist nicht mehr gegeben. Ein eindringliches Beispiel für ein uneingeschränktes Handlungsspiel begegnet uns in der Aufnahme *Fifth Avenue 3, 2009*. Ganz rechts im Bild lehnt an der Wand eines Hochhauses ein Mann mit einer Einkaufstüte und sonnt sich für einen Moment. Seinen Schatten links sehen wir in einer geradezu fantastischen Ausdehnung, die sich über den von ihm besetzten Architekturabschnitt erstreckt. Weitergeführt wird dieser Schatten von der links an diesem jungen Mann vorbeigehenden Dame im hellen Mantel. Von ihrem linken Fuß aus nehmen wir einen lang gezogenen Schatten auf dem Bürgersteig wahr, der auch ihre Gehrichtung markiert und in Richtung des Ladeneingangs führt.

Diese – hier explizierten – präzisen Beobachtungen verdeutlichen das Kunstwollen von Gudrun Kemsa. Es ist der schöne Schein dieser Welt Manhattans, symbolisiert durch die prächtige Fifth Avenue, die immer wieder herausgehoben wird. In diese sehr aufgeräumte Welt passen keine Schmutzgegenstände, die von der Fotografin konsequenterweise wegretuschiert werden. Der

schöne Schein existiert in deutlicher Gegenwart. Das Wort *Schein* leitet sich bekanntlich vom mittelhochdeutschen *schîn* ab, wobei wir heute diesen Begriff mit *Glanz* oder auch *Lichterscheinung* übersetzen. Diese Erscheinungen des Lichtes, in Kooperation mit der machtvollen Geometrie von Architekturgebäuden und dem Bewegungsimpuls der Agierenden, gehören zum Alphabet der Künstlerin, die uns das urbane Leben in den Metropolen auf spezifische Weise nahebringt. Sie ist die Regisseurin, die uns eine Wirklichkeit nach ihrer Vorstellung präsentiert. Gebäude, vorbeigehende Menschen etc. existieren ohne Zweifel, das Zusammenspiel aller bildet die Synthese dieser Kunst. Der schöne Schein ist das Gegenstück zur begrifflichen Realität bzw. zur Wahrheit. Selbstverständlich übt der schöne Schein eine ungemeine Faszination auf die Menschen aus. Ohne ihn gäbe es vermutlich keine Kunst, zumal keine im westlichen Sinne. Durch das 20. Jahrhundert hindurch wurde das Schöne immer wieder durch Hässlichkeit oder Zerstörung gebrochen. Auch in unserer Gegenwart steht Ästhetik, einst eine profunde Beschäftigung mit der Bedingung des Schönen, unter Generalverdacht. Das Schöne ist im Allgemeinen kein Leitmotiv des Schaffens mehr. Gudrun Kemsa kehrt diese Verdrehung mit der ihr eigenen Bildsprache um. Ihre Augenblicksrealität fasziniert.

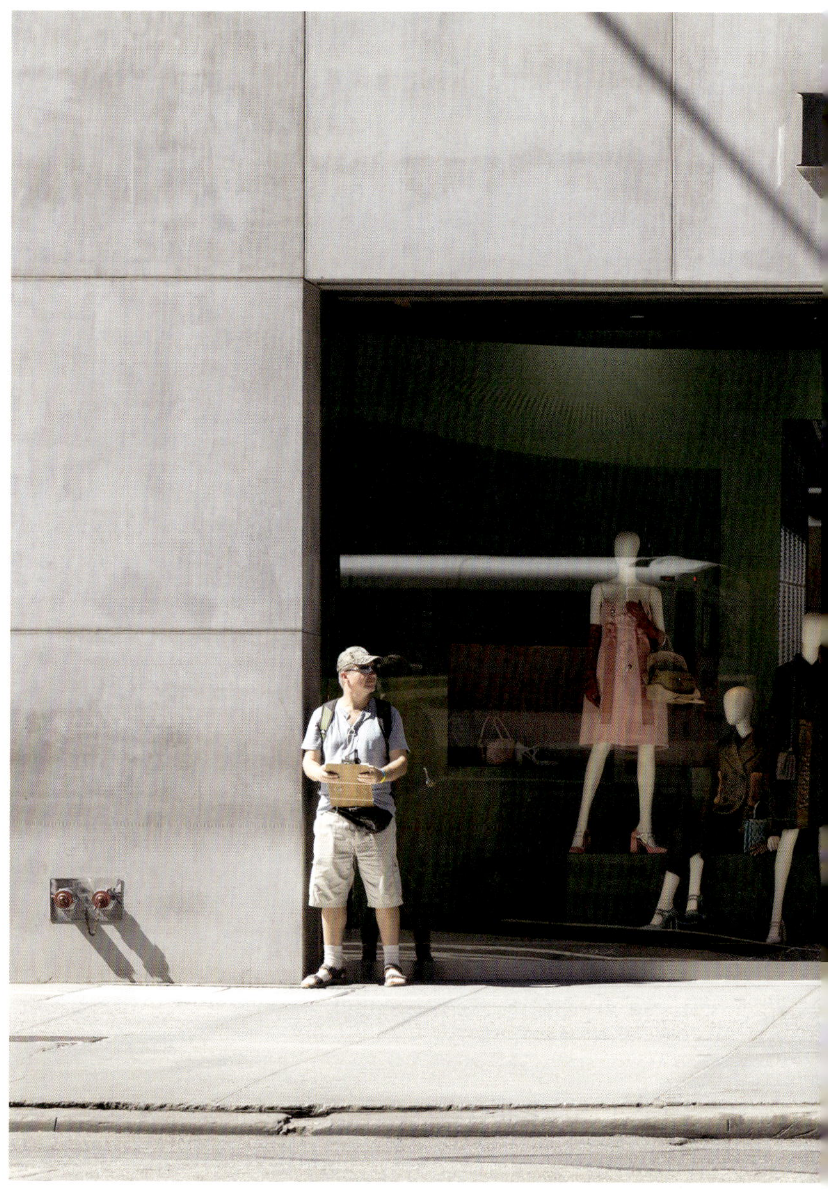

    42nd Street 3, 2018

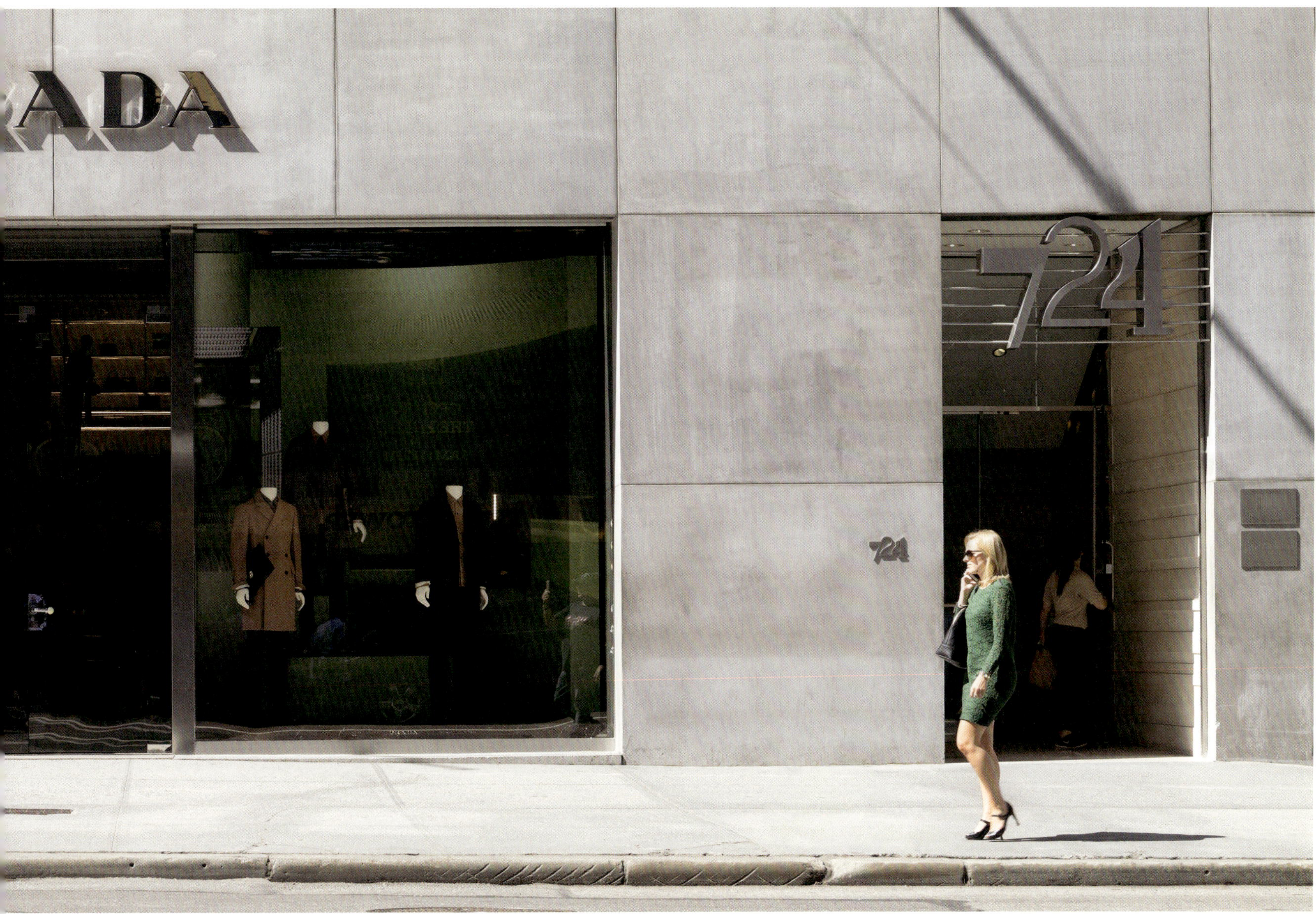

ADA
724
724

"My counterpart is my motif"
Remarks on Gudrun Kemsa's New York Pictures
by Tayfun Belgin

In a short text connected with the picture series *Manhattan*, the artist makes the following statement:

> *Urban architecture becomes a stage on which the protagonists act. The light in Manhattan is bright and clear and it seems almost as if it was only created to perfectly illuminate the whole scenery of this huge stage in a natural way...*

Particularly in cities, the world is a stage on which infinite performances of people moving purposefully or casually and freely take place each day. Reality occurs in the plural; we never obtain just one single picture of this world. Everything is in a state of flux, as the pre-Socratics taught us. Everything fluctuates, and nothing remains; there is only an eternal becoming and changing. Time and movement thus become our constants. The pictures visualize in their way what we conceptualize as movement and impermanence. Beyond coincidence, one conceptual inspiration for Gudrun Kemsa might have been when she decided to generate moving pictures with her photography. In the photos, again and again we encounter individuals who walk quickly or slowly, turn around, stand still, meet others, and stop at a traffic light at some point, to then start moving again a short time later.

Gudrun Kemsa observes. She has a counterpart. That is her motif. She is the one side; her counterpart is the other. She observes while others take action: a peculiar asymmetry, Niklas Luhmann would say. Silent observer and moving partner, whereby the latter become the actor in these pictures quite involuntarily. Gudrun Kemsa has visited New York repeatedly, and, indeed, at very different times. That Midtown in particular delights nearly all visitors to the city is clear. We find ourselves in the center of high capitalism. This part of New York generates pictures of at times endless beauty on its streets and squares. Another part of this island that never sleeps reveals a totally different, very specific aesthetic: Downtown, Little Italy, or Harlem—these parts of the city are also frequently photographed and found in innumerable films. But they inspire narratives that are not Gudrun Kemsa's focus. These areas are where myths of heroes, mafia bosses, and brilliant jazz musicians develop—narratives that have provided material for all kinds of films, from romantic movies to brutal gangster films. New York offers the best place in the United States for exaggerations and neuroses, from Wall Street to Woody Allen's favorite film locations.

Gudrun Kemsa's observant eye perceives actions that we miss due to a lack of time or interest. We do not see her motifs, or to put it more correctly: we do not perceive what happens on the street with her eyes. To participate in these fluid worlds, which do not produce any substance, one needs time. When time is available, the play with the ephemeral world of the street becomes more fascinating. Time is the condition for Gudrun Kemsa's photography. We as viewers generally pass by the stagings that the photographer effects. But she masters the principle of juxtaposition and connection. Gudrun Kemsa observes the opposite side of the street with concentration, and waits until people she does not know come together and provide her with a motif for a picture. At this moment, they are eternalized by her briefly pressing the shutter release.

Concretely: in the picture *42nd Street 3, 2018*, two people who perhaps do not know each other meet on the sidewalk in front of a Prada store. On the left edge of the display window, a man is looking to the right at an elegantly dressed woman walking toward him. It is this decisive moment, to use the words of Cartier-Bresson, that inspired Gudrun Kemsa to take a photograph of the two people, neither of whom she knows. Both individuals—the male tourist with a cap and 3/4-length trousers on the left, and the female New Yorker dressed in a green dress and talking on her cellphone—are actors in front of a massive concrete architecture at the moment they are photographed. They emphasize the vertical dimension of the building. When the woman on the telephone has nearly reached the Prada store, another woman is standing behind her on the right, still within the frame of the entrance area of building No. 724. A man is standing on the left, vertical edge of the store. The shop with its display of mannequins is itself quasi inlaid in this bright concrete architecture. A principle in Gudrun Kemsa's photography today is revealed here: she composes her photographs with baselines, with verticals and horizontals. They are supplemented with windows as frames for passersby and door entrances with a strict geometry, which serve as master axes: traffic lights, columns, a bus stop with an information stele, lamps hanging down on buildings, and so on.

Photos that do not have a "flat" counterpart of an architecture as a basic motif but instead show a corner situation require a differentiated look. On the one hand, a different depth is offered here; on the other, the framework for action is expanded. People walk from left to right and vice versa, cross the street at traffic lights, or stand still for a short moment. The large store situated behind them does not have as much presence anymore. Here, one might ask whether a narrative structure is inherent in this kind of street photography. What can be determined is that we have an image that reproduces a happening in these pictures. But this is not a classical narrative, since there is no actor relating something. Here, people who do not know each other encounter one another on the street, or on steps in the subway, and are reported on visually at a particular moment. In the series of pictures *Subway* of 2018, the coincidences are emphasized even more strongly. Here, in the subsurface of the city, the anonymity seems to be even greater than up on the street.

With respect to the three classical units of time, space, and action, which Aristotle considered necessary in a drama, we find a correlation in the pictures of Gudrun Kemsa. The people photographed find themselves at the same place at a particular time, and take action. At the same time, no drama in five acts can be retraced in these pictures; the basic tenor is instead the ephemeral. It is therefore not possible to speak of the concept of narration in the classical sense, since what we are dealing with here is a non-binding narrative. The photo brings together people who could be part of a narrative at this moment. At the moment the shutter is released, each figure takes on a specific role. There are individuals standing, walking, waiting, reading, and so on. All are in one picture, but a narrative about all of them is not provided; they are merely portrayed.

Everything that is depicted participates in a world dedicated to outer appearances, including the fantastic stores on prestigious Fifth Avenue and the grand architecture, which we also find in Paris (La Défense), Berlin, London, or Dubai. Gudrun Kemsa has made her way to all these places and partaken of their respective atmospheres. She did not photograph a situation in rainy weather at any of the locations, and definitely not at Venice Beach or Al Merraija (Dubai). Rain is not part of this photo-graphy. When it rains, people sometimes act in a frenzied way and are—above all in industrial nations—rather impatient. Sovereignty of movement is impaired; the freedom that Gudrun Kemsa captures in her actors is no longer a given. We encounter a salient example of unimpaired scope for action in the photo *5th Avenue 3, 2009*. At the far right of the picture, a man is leaning on the wall of a high-rise building, holding a shopping bag and sunning himself for a moment. We see his shadow extending toward the left in an almost fantastical way, stretching over the section of the architecture that he occupies. The woman in a light-colored coat walking past this young man from the left continues this shadow. From her left foot, we see an elongated shadow on the sidewalk, which also marks her walking direction and leads toward the entrance of a shop.

The precise observations explicated here exemplify Gudrun Kemsa's artistic intentions. It is the beautiful appearance of this world of Manhattan symbolized by magnificent Fifth Avenue that is highlighted again and again. No dirty objects, all of which the photographer consistently retouches, fit into this immaculately tidy world. The beautiful appearance exists in a distinct present. The German word for appearance, *Schein*, is derived, as is generally known, from the Middle German *schîn*, so that today this term is translated as *shine* or *light phenomenon*. These light phenomena, along with the powerful geometry of buildings and the movement impulses of the protagonists, are part of the artist's alphabet for bringing us closer to the urban life in metropolises in a specific way. She is the director who presents reality to us based on her imagination. Buildings, passersby, and so forth undoubtedly exist; it is the interplay of all this that gives rise to the synthesis of this art. Beautiful appearances are the counterpart to the conceptual reality and/or truth. People are naturally fascinated by beautiful appearances. Without such appearances, there would probably not be any art, particularly not in the Western sense. Throughout the twentieth century, beauty was repeatedly fractured by ugliness or destruction. Aesthetics, once a profound engagement with the conditions of the beautiful, are also regarded with general suspicion in our present. The beautiful is no longer a general guiding principle for creativity. Gudrun Kemsa inverts this distortion with her own visual vocabulary. Her reality of the moment fascinates.

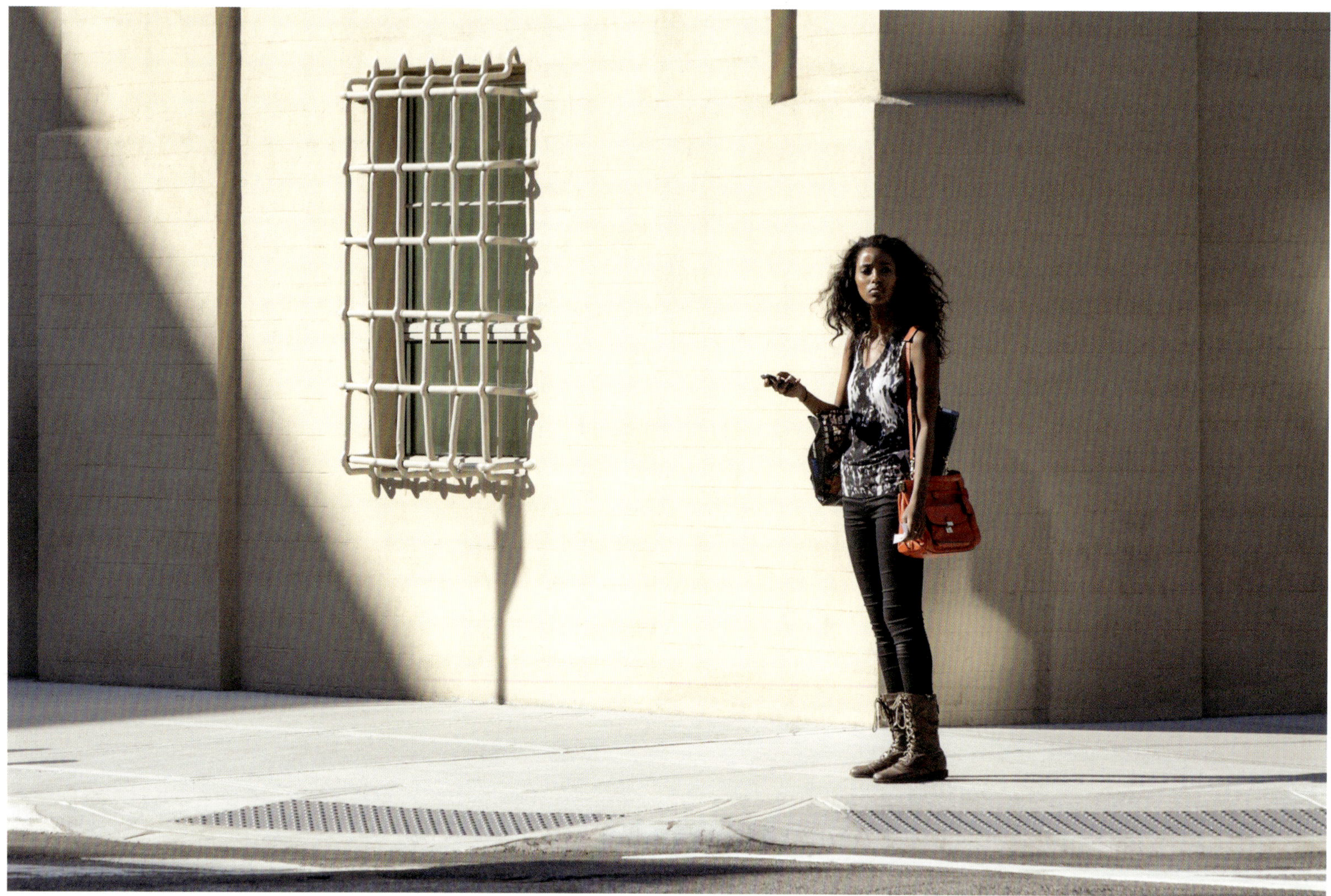

     10th Avenue 6, 2016

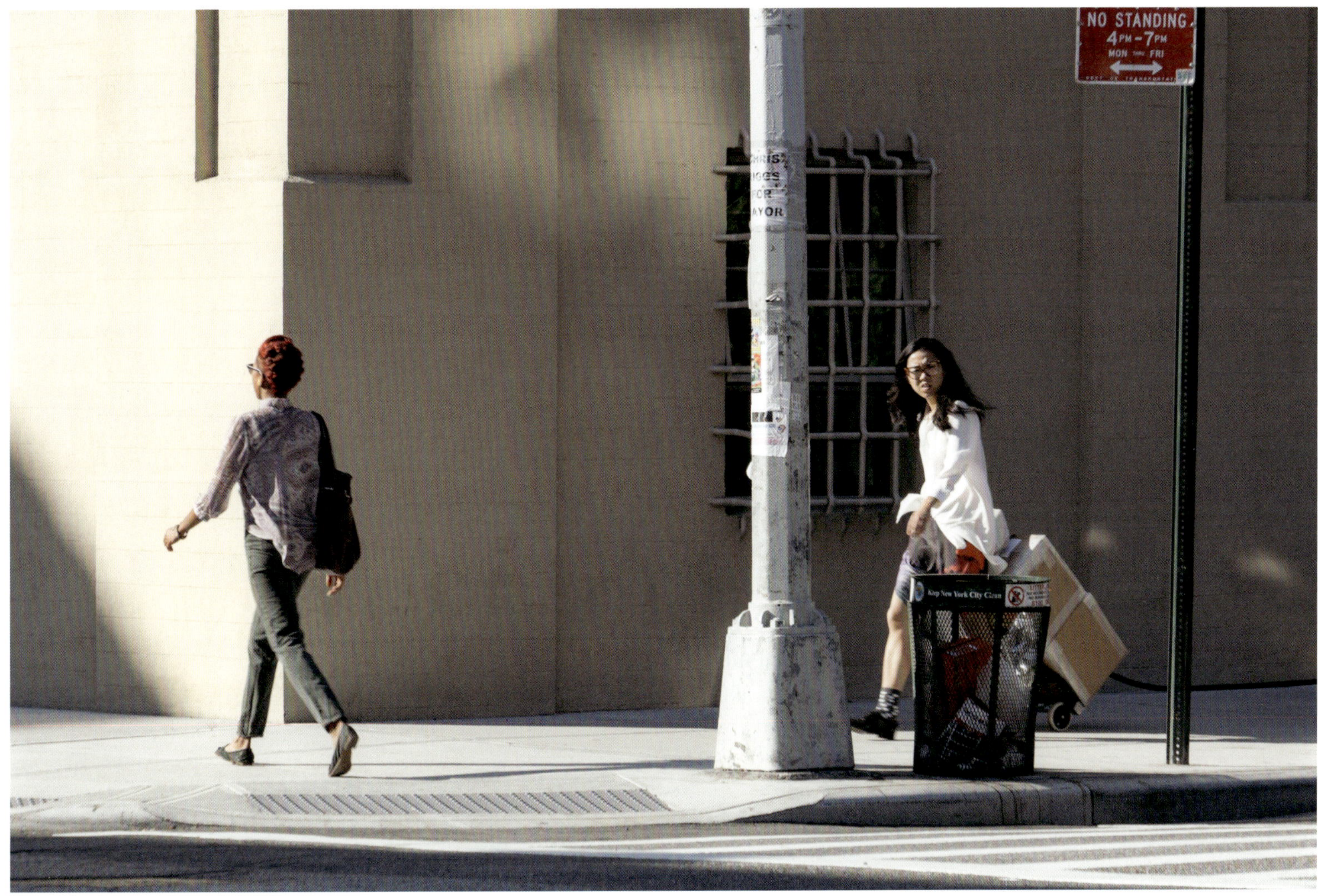

10th Avenue 5, 2016   15

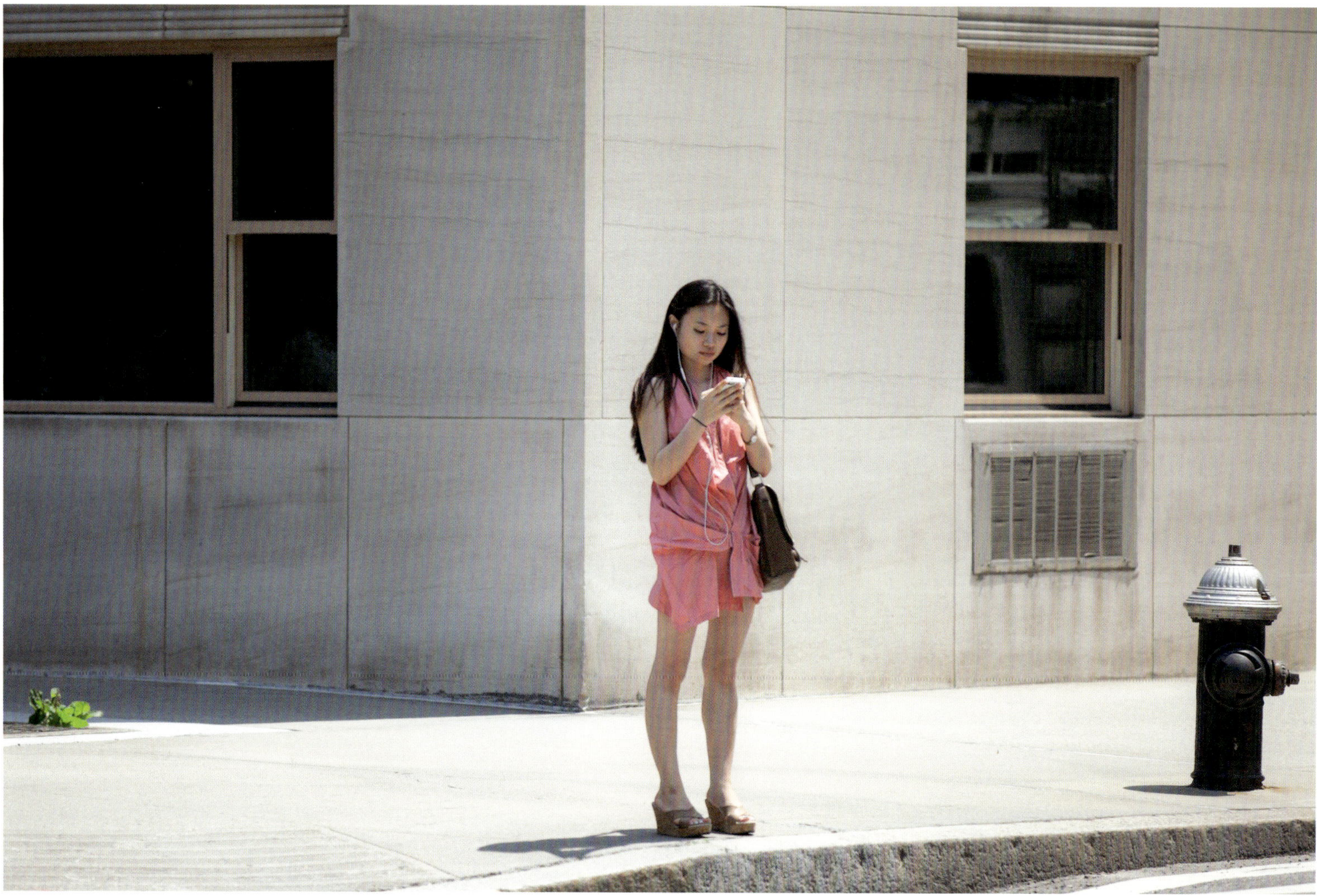

16   5th Avenue 20, 2016

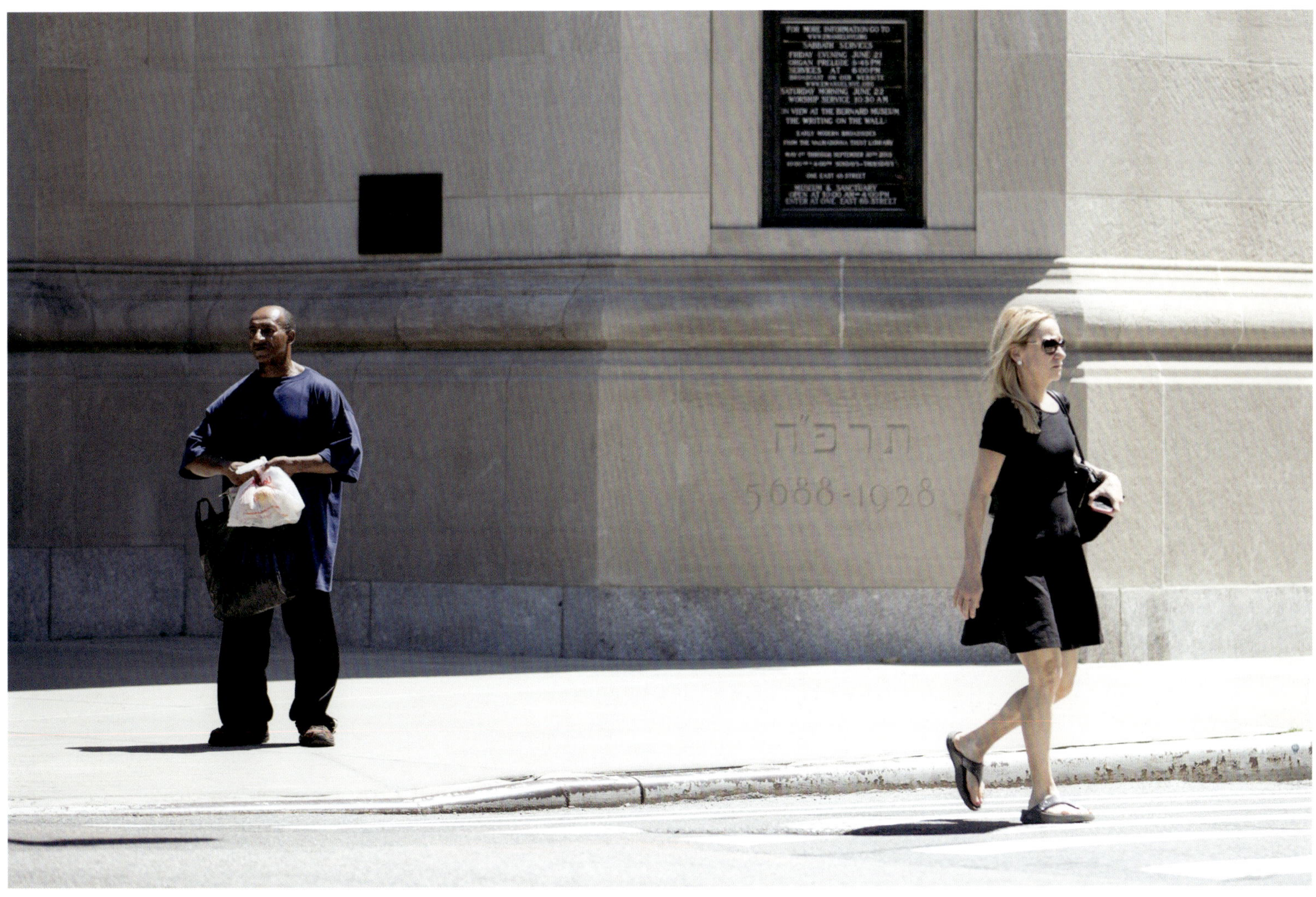

5688-1928

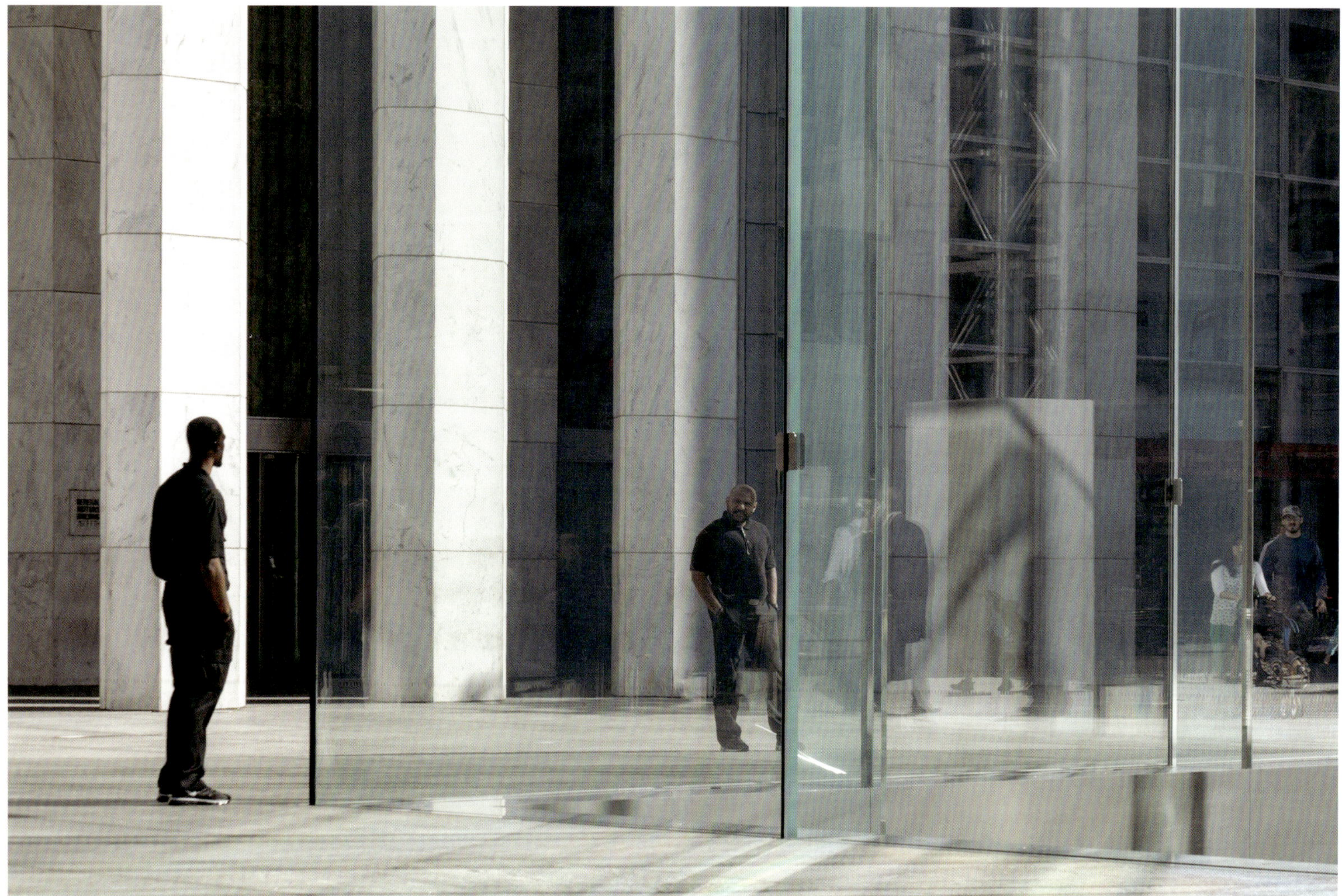

    Apple Store 1, 2016

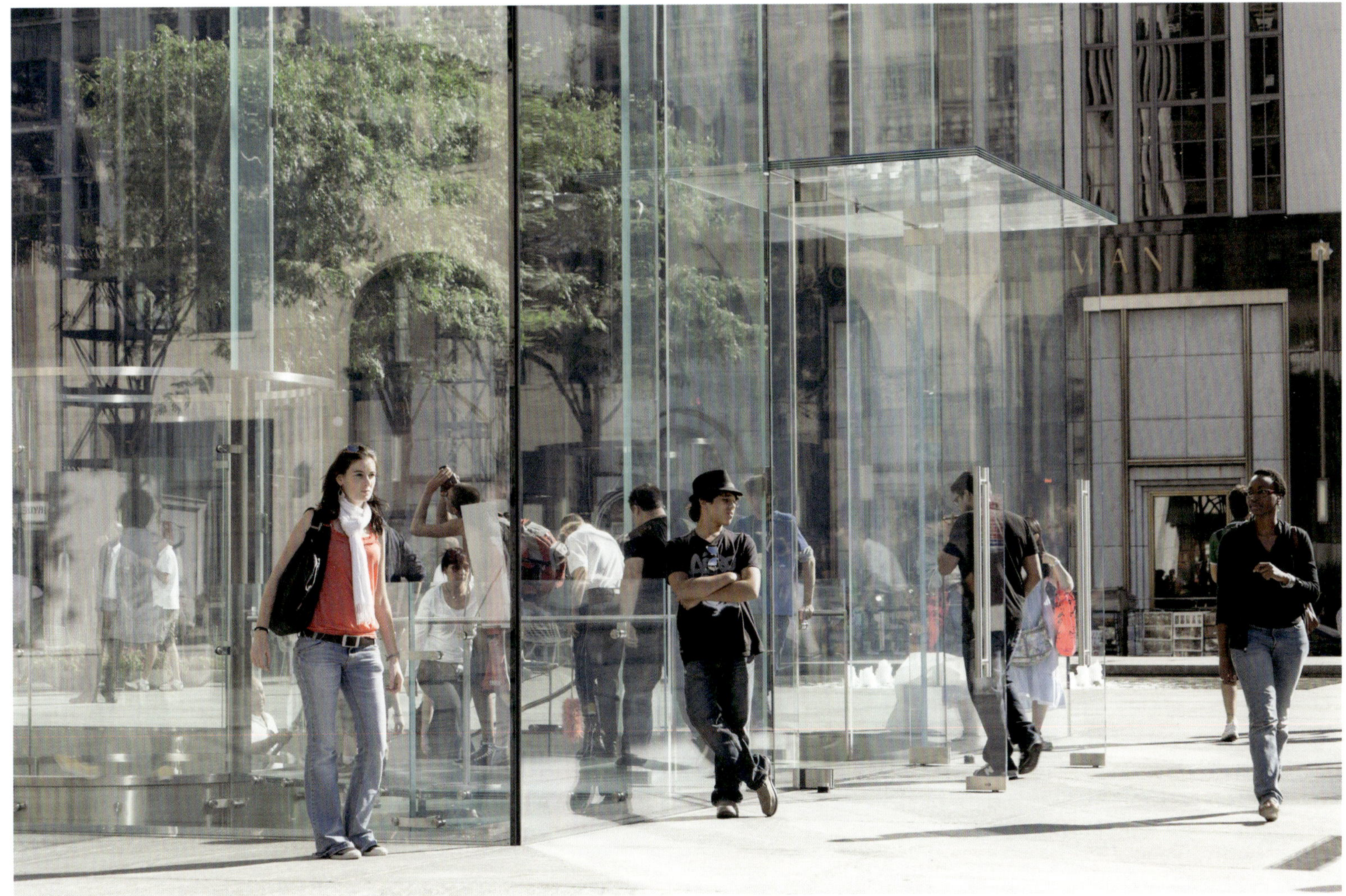

Apple Store 2, 2016   19

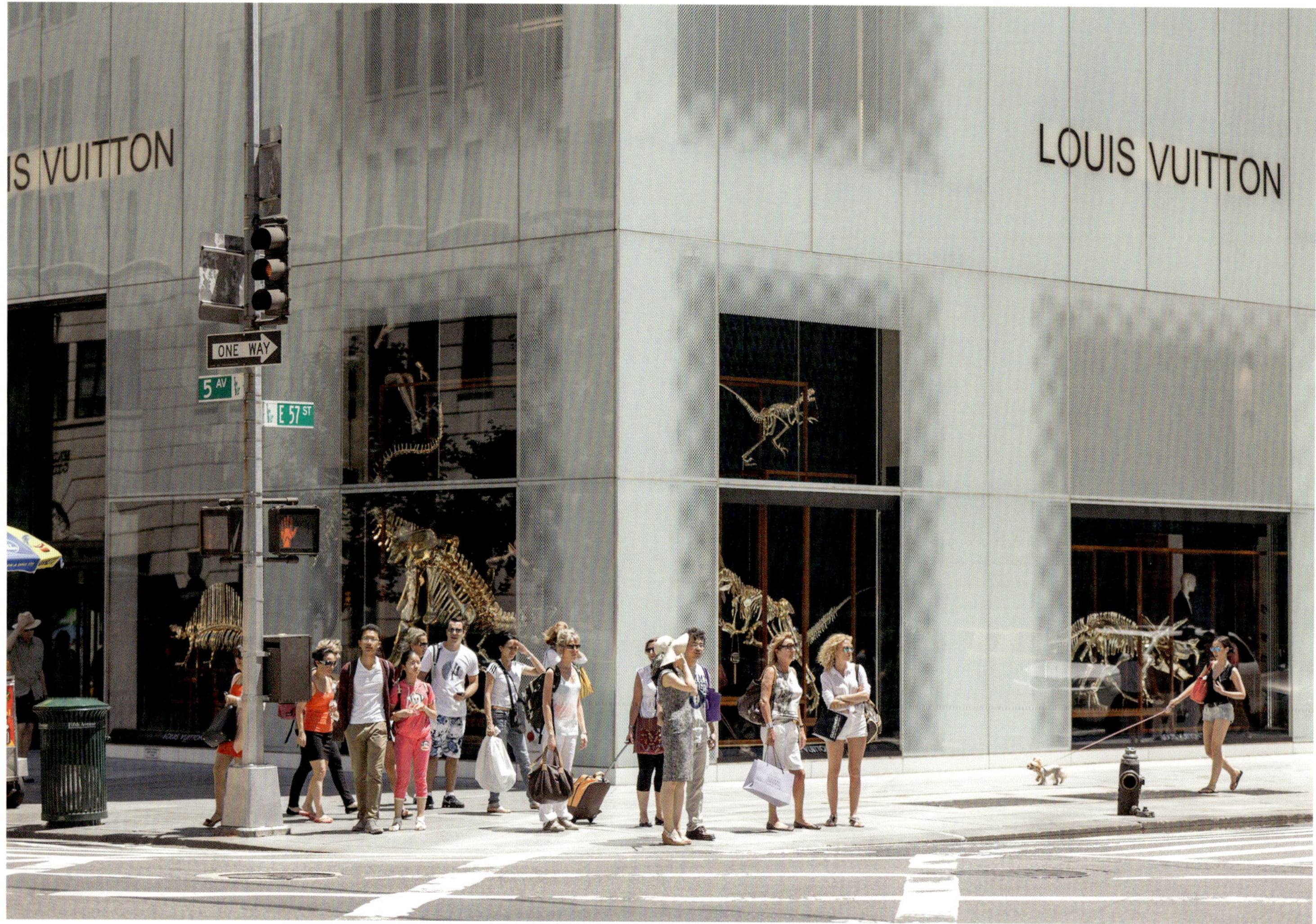

    5th Avenue 23, 2013

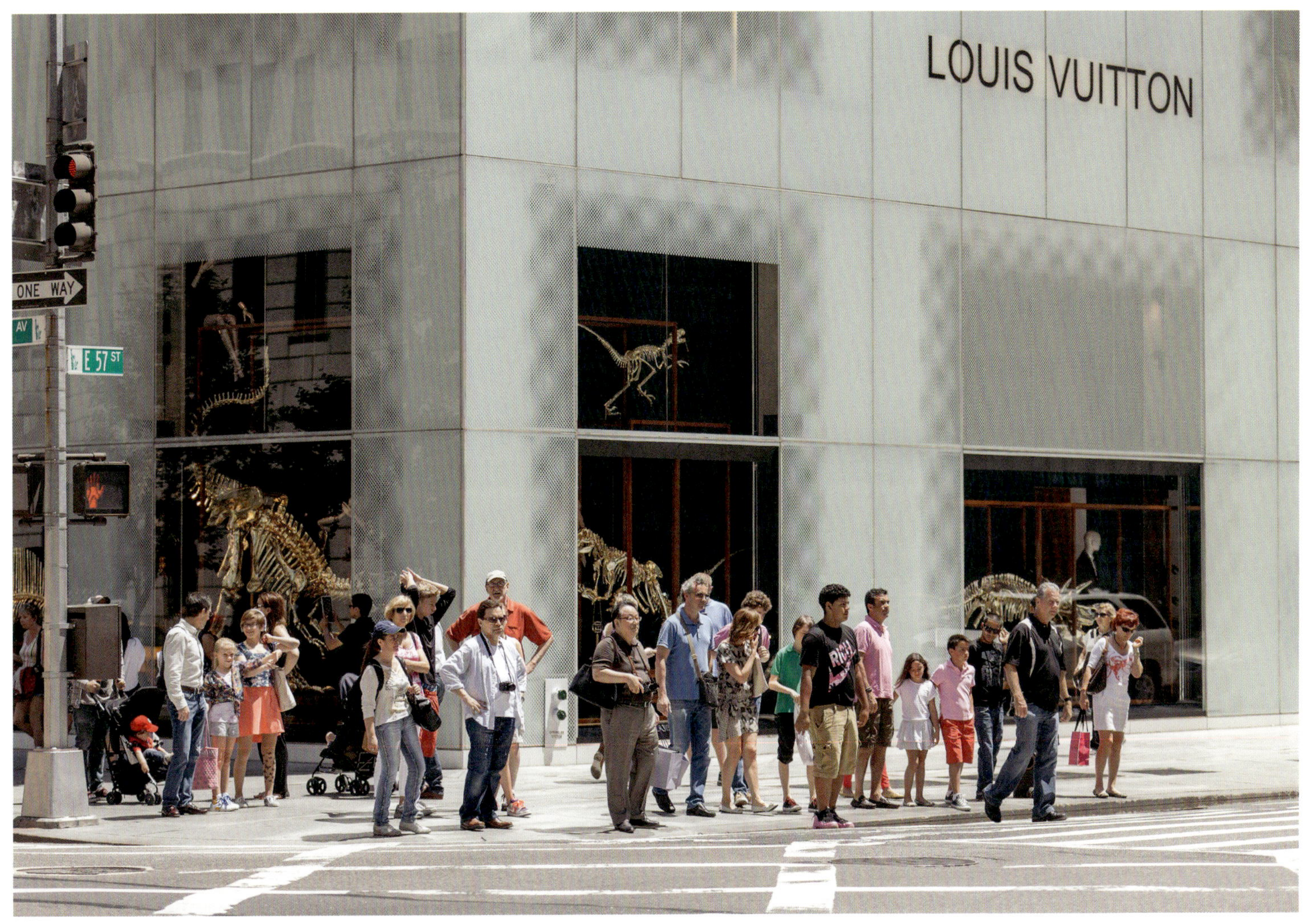

LOUIS VUITTON
ONE WAY
AV
E 57 ST

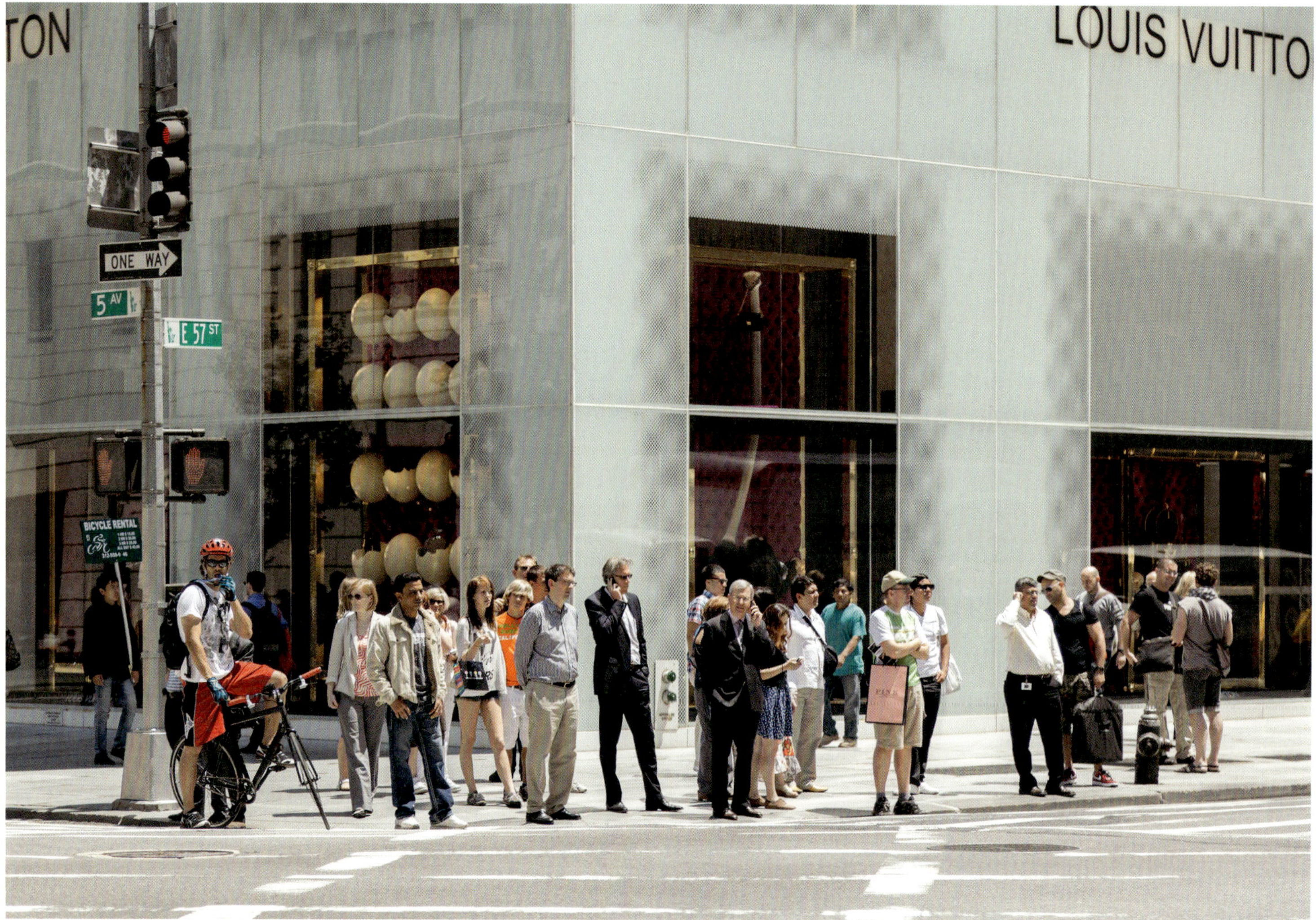

     5th Avenue 57, 2011

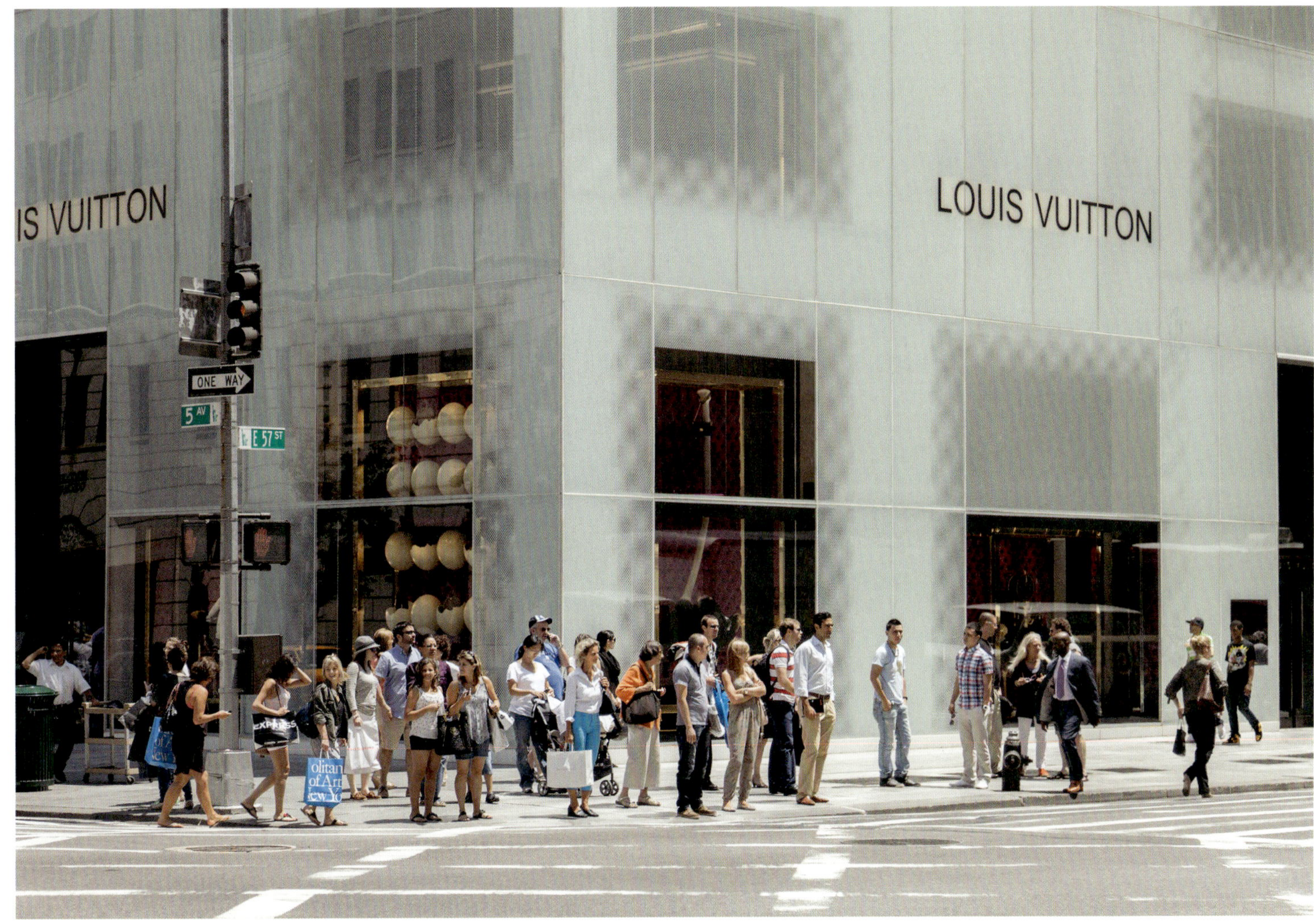

5th Avenue 60, 2011   23

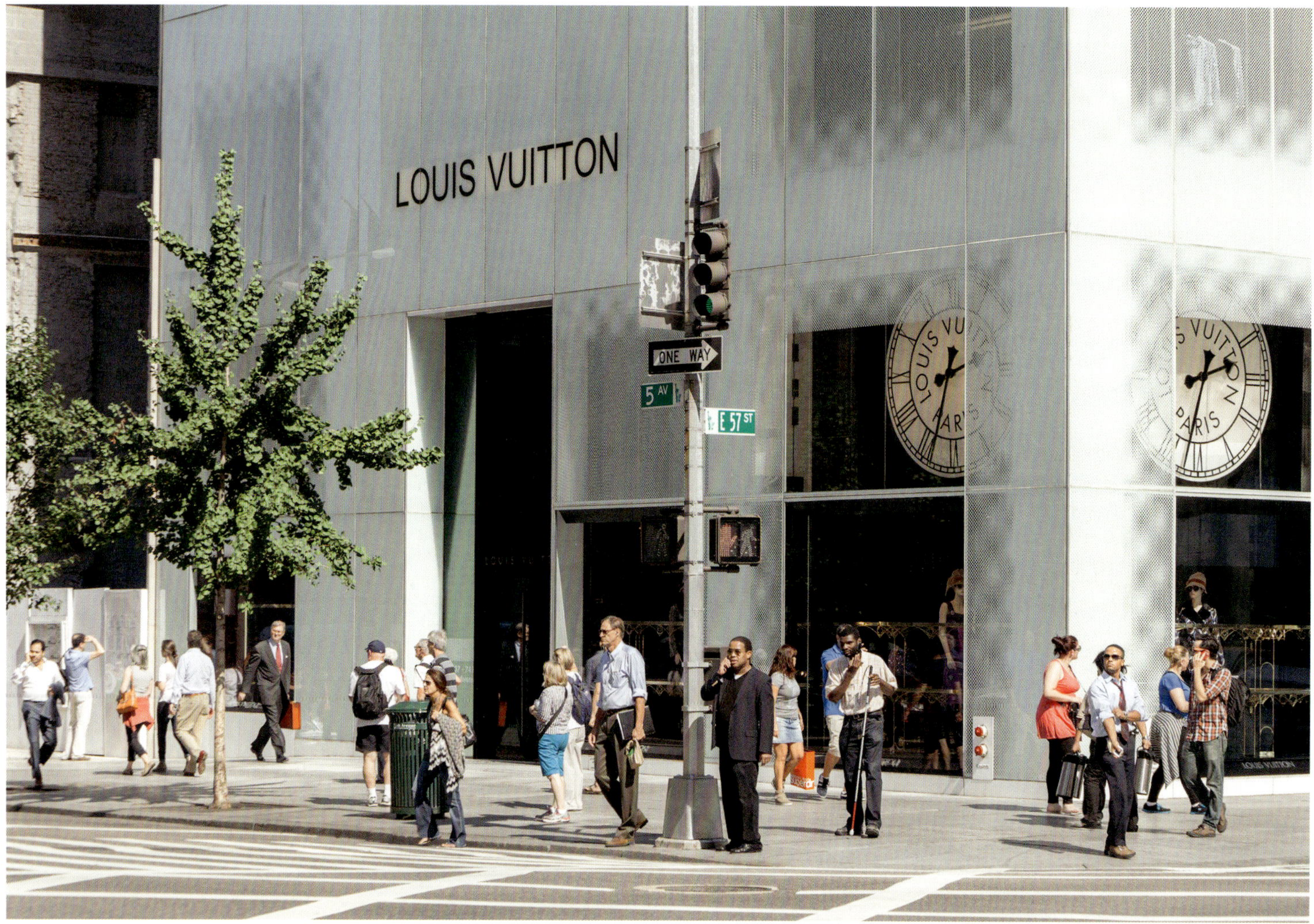

24   5th Avenue 5, 2012

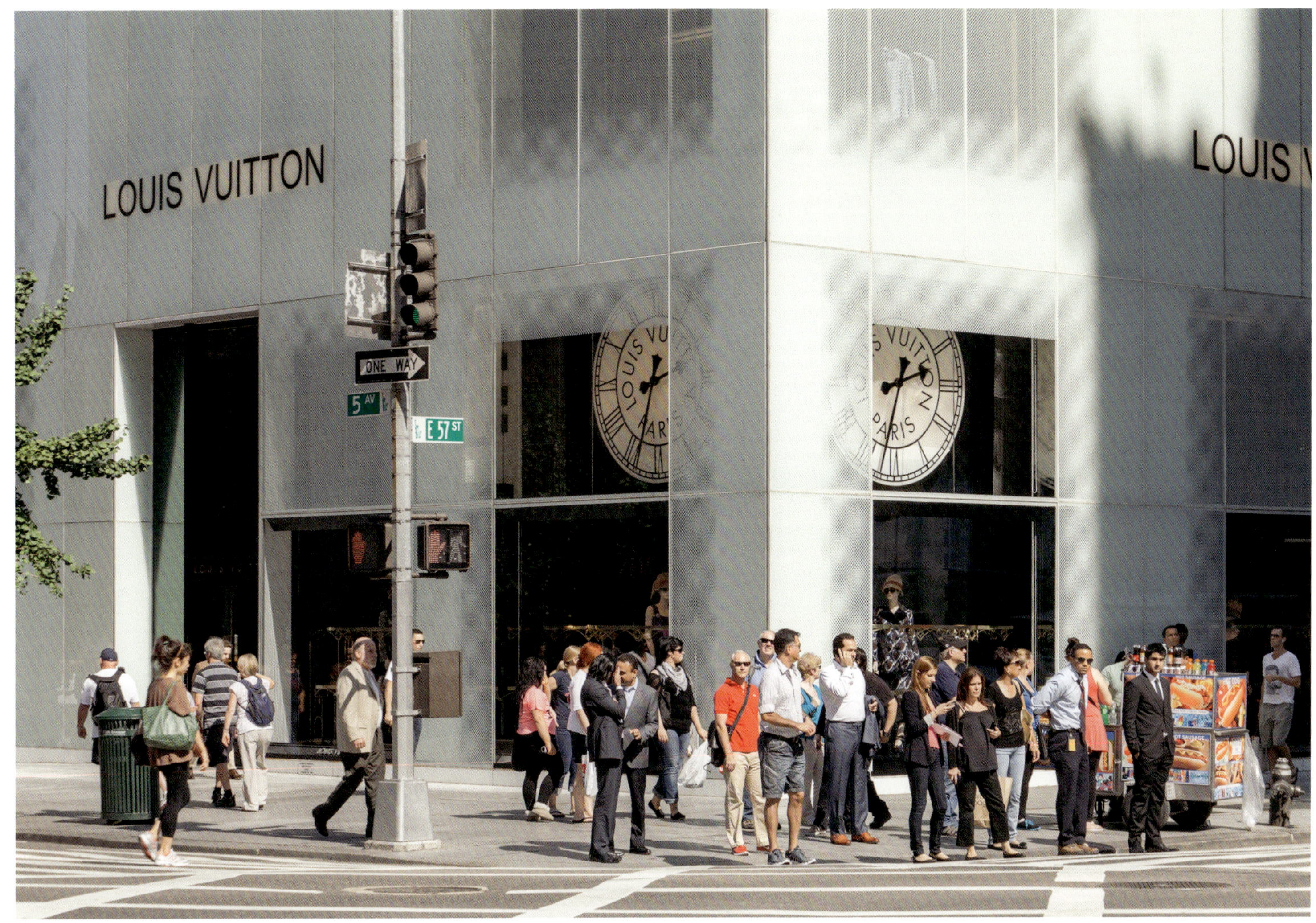
LOUIS VUITTON
LOUIS V
ONE WAY
5 AV
E 57 ST
LOUIS VUITTON PARIS
LOUIS VUITTON PARIS

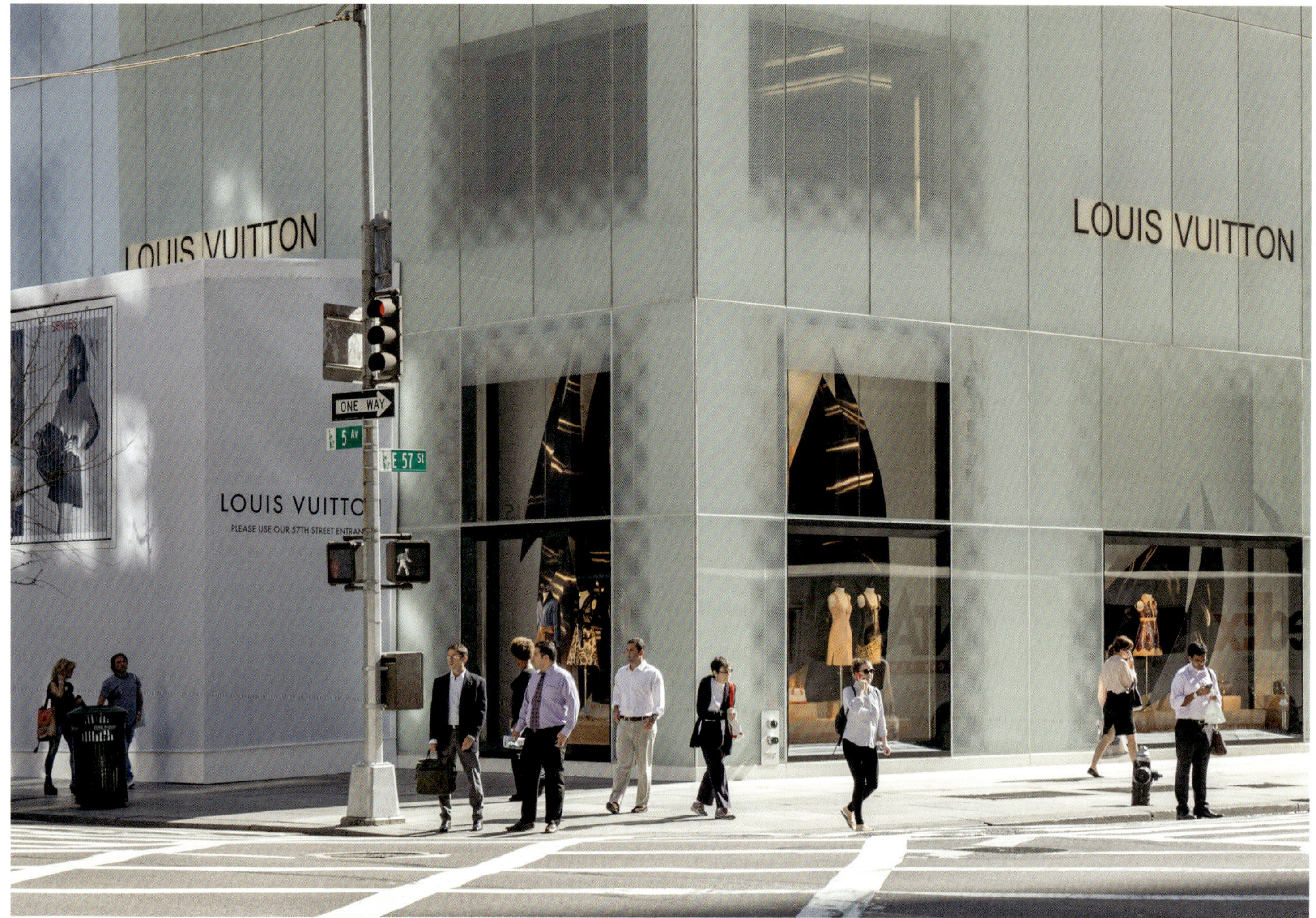

26 5th Avenue 51, 2014

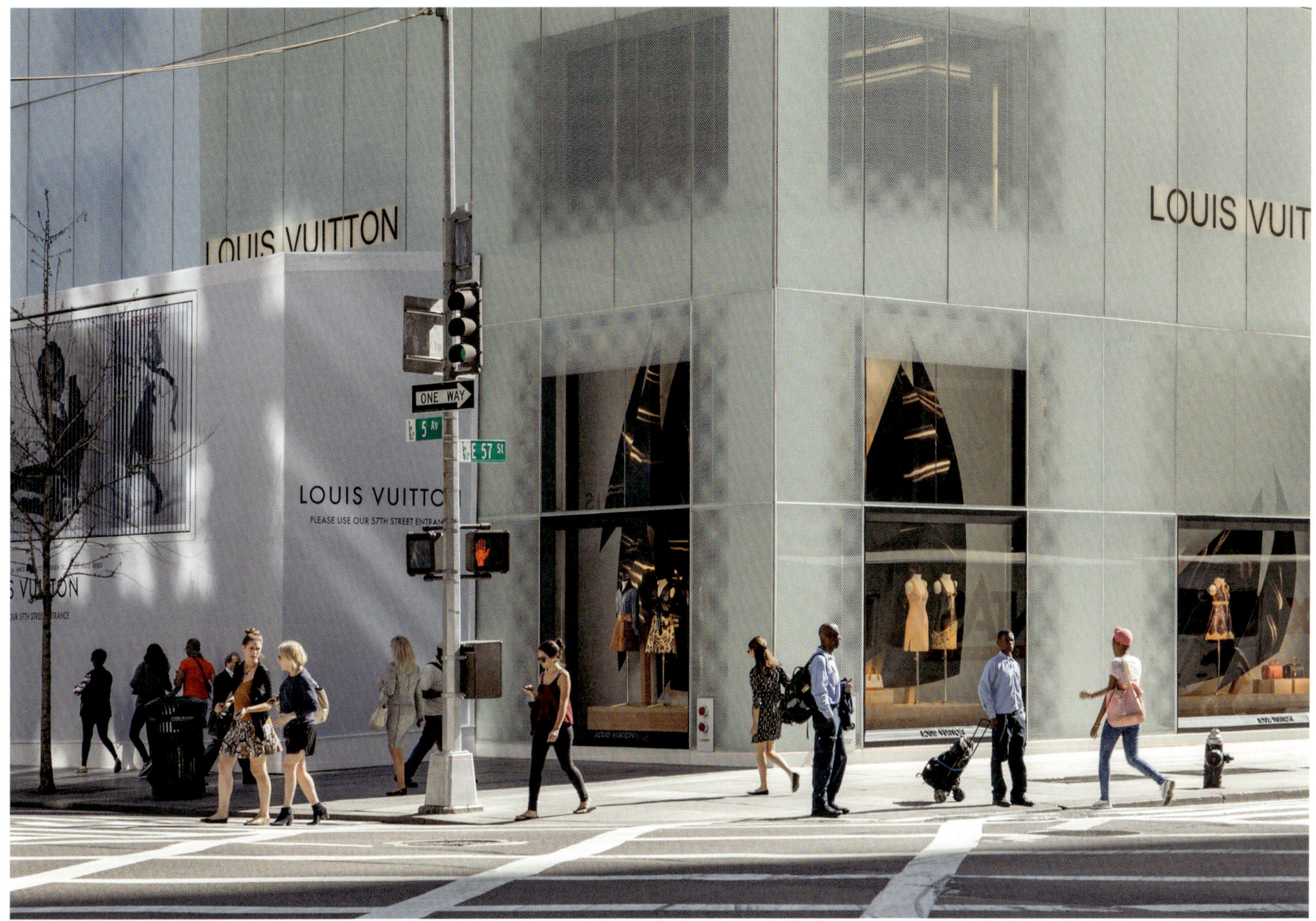

LOUIS VUITTON
LOUIS VUITTON
LOUIS VUITTON
PLEASE USE OUR 57TH STREET ENTRANCE
ONE WAY
5 AV
E 57 St

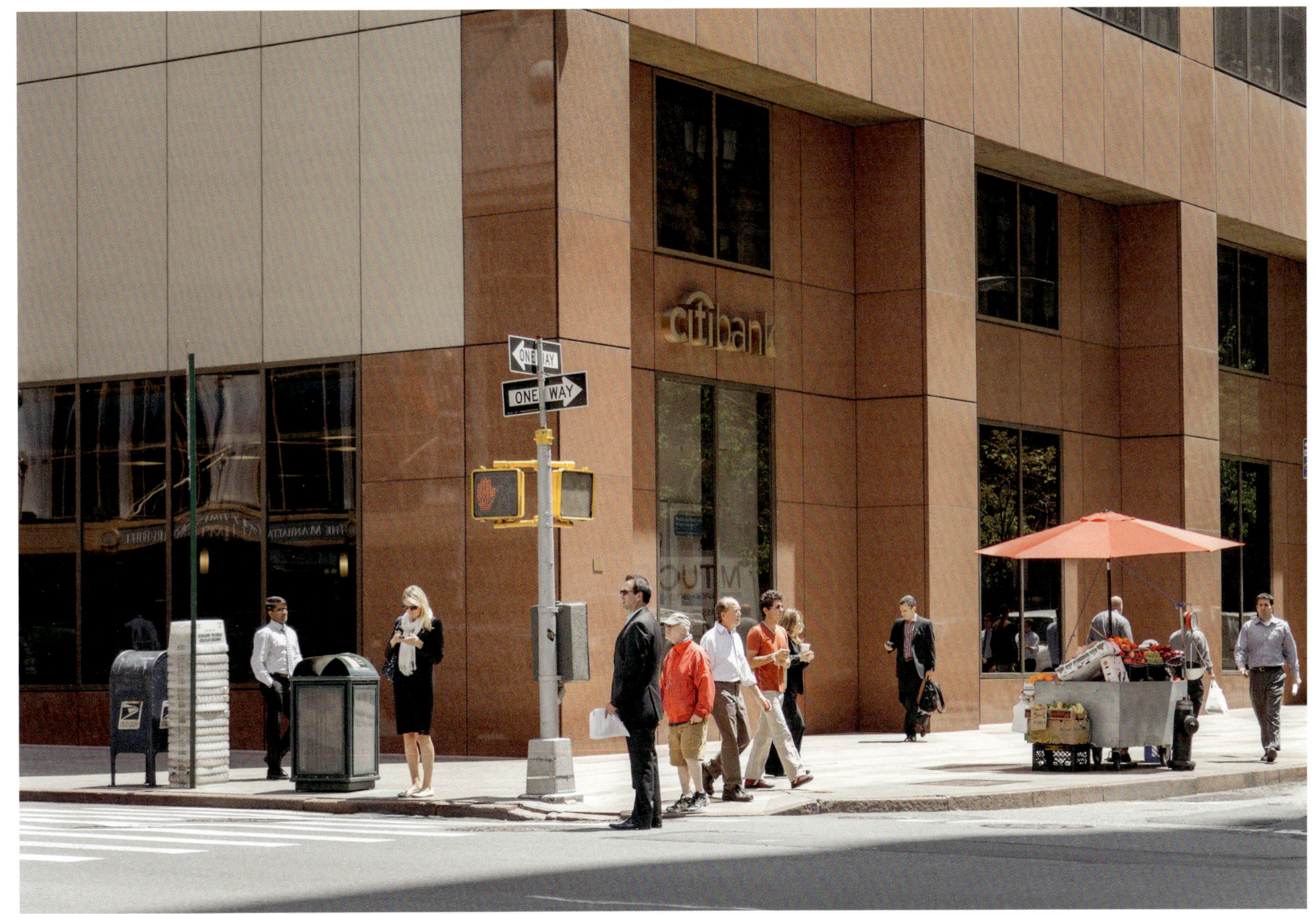

7th Avenue 1, 2011   29

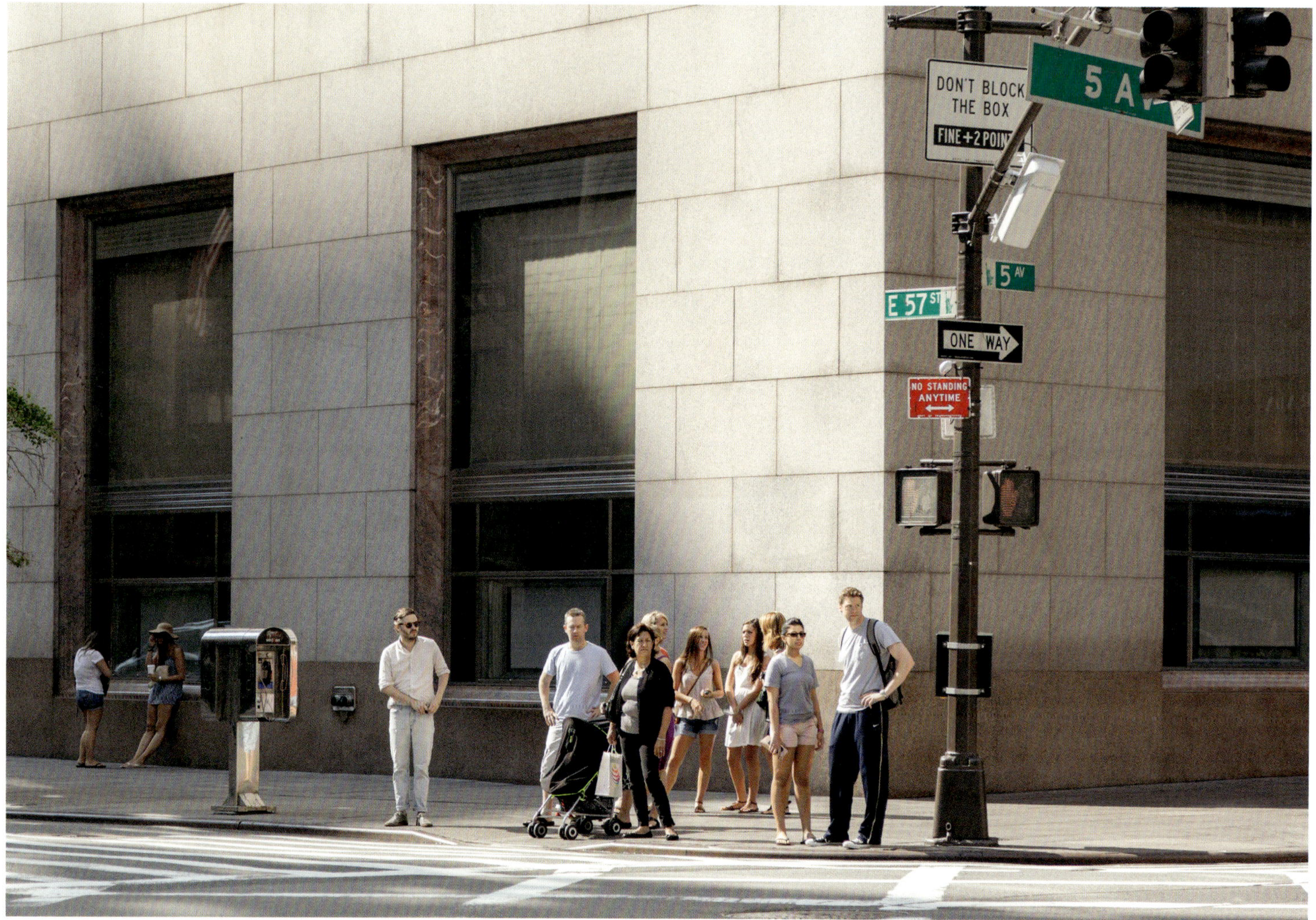

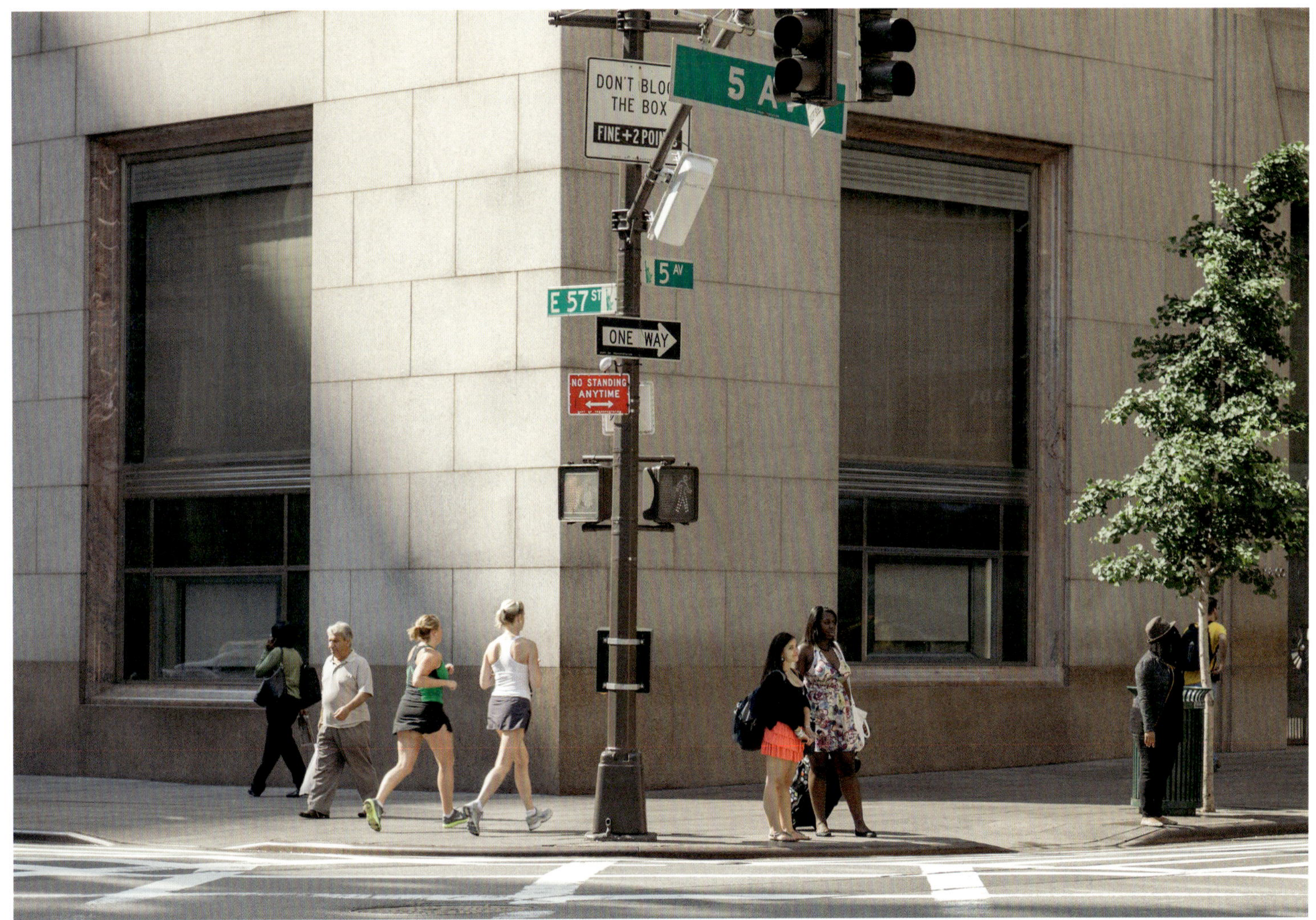

DON'T BLOCK
THE BOX
FINE +2 POINTS
5 AV
5 AV
E 57 ST
ONE WAY
NO STANDING
ANYTIME

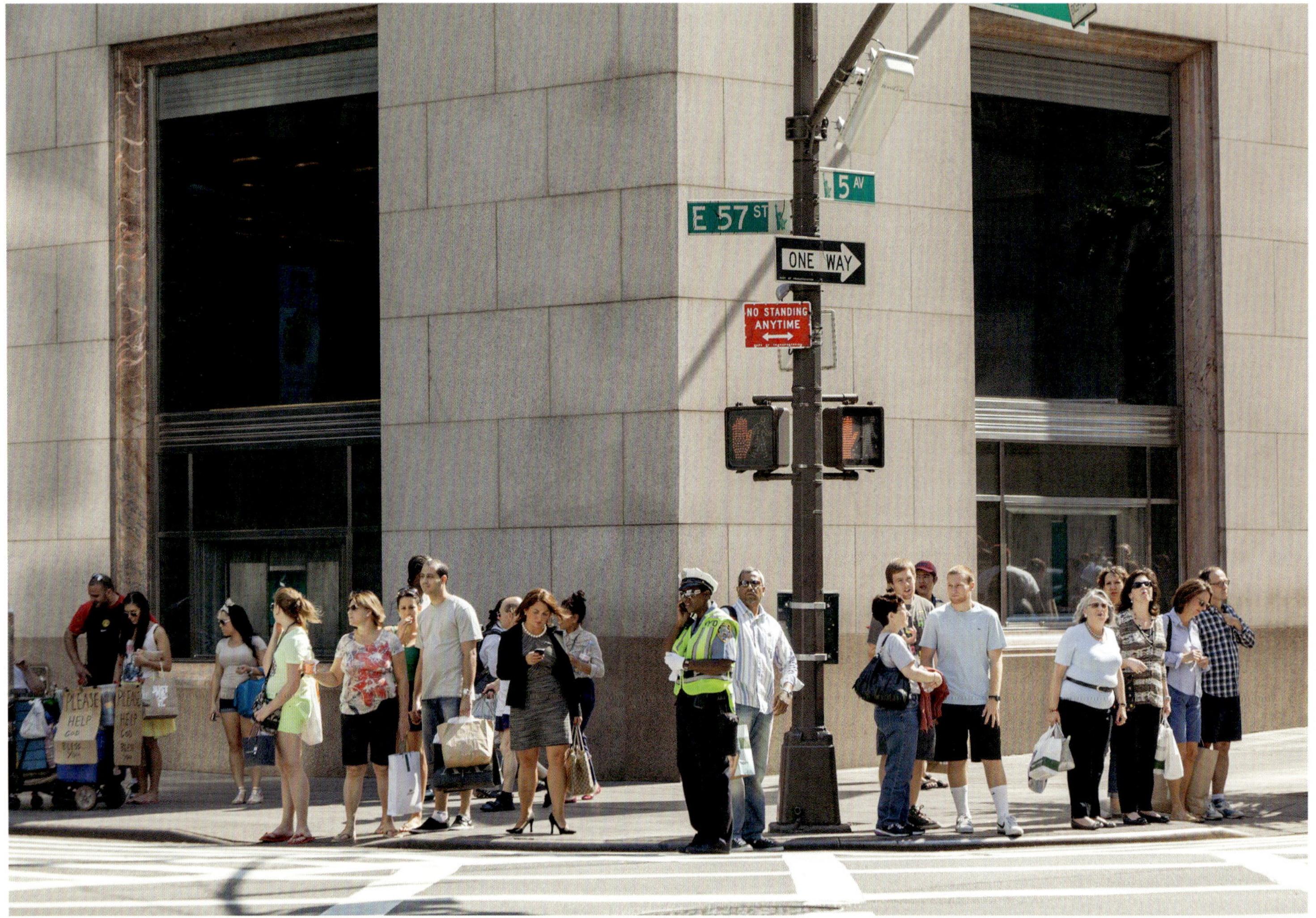

32   5th Avenue 66, 2012

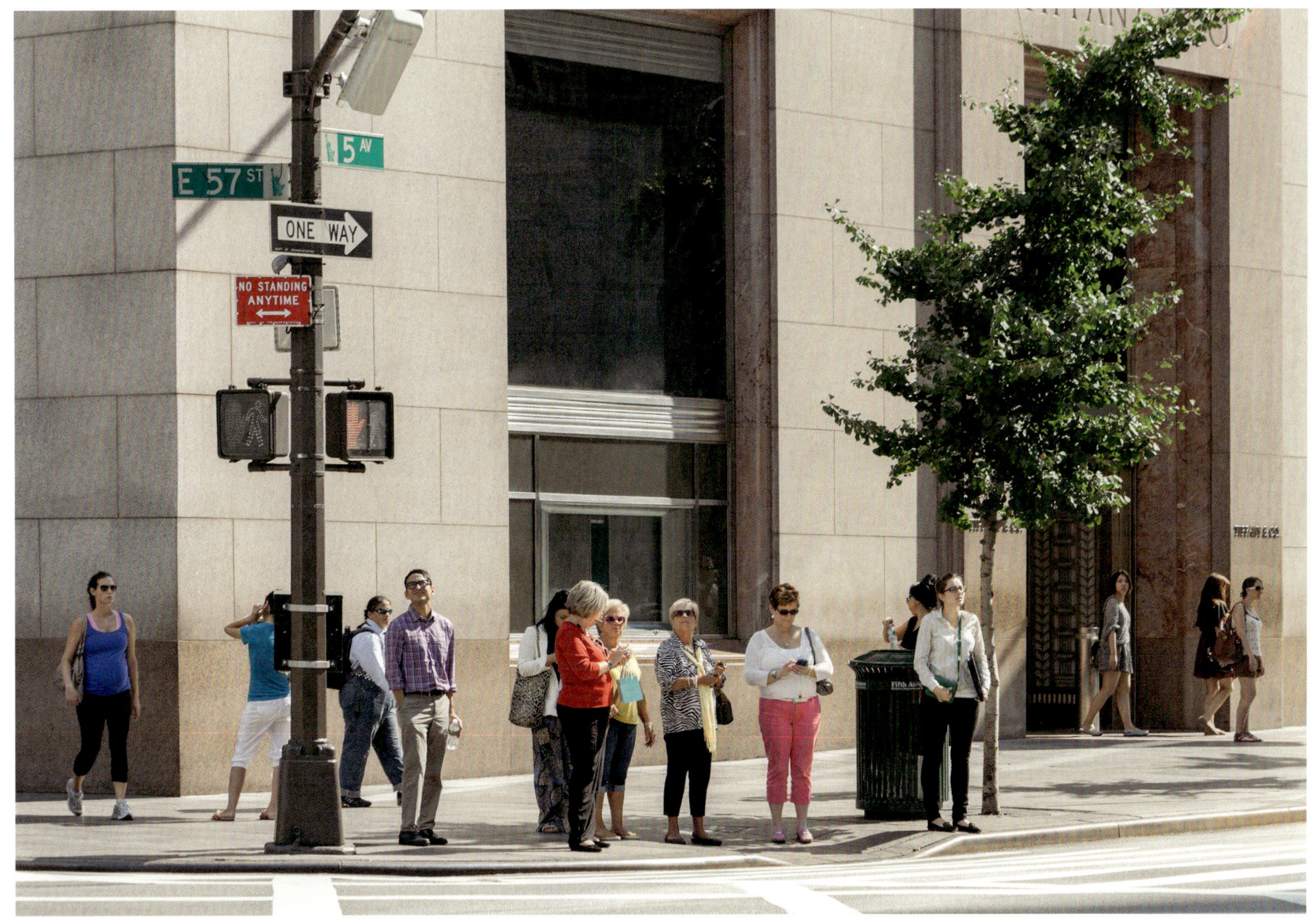

5th Avenue 70, 2012   33

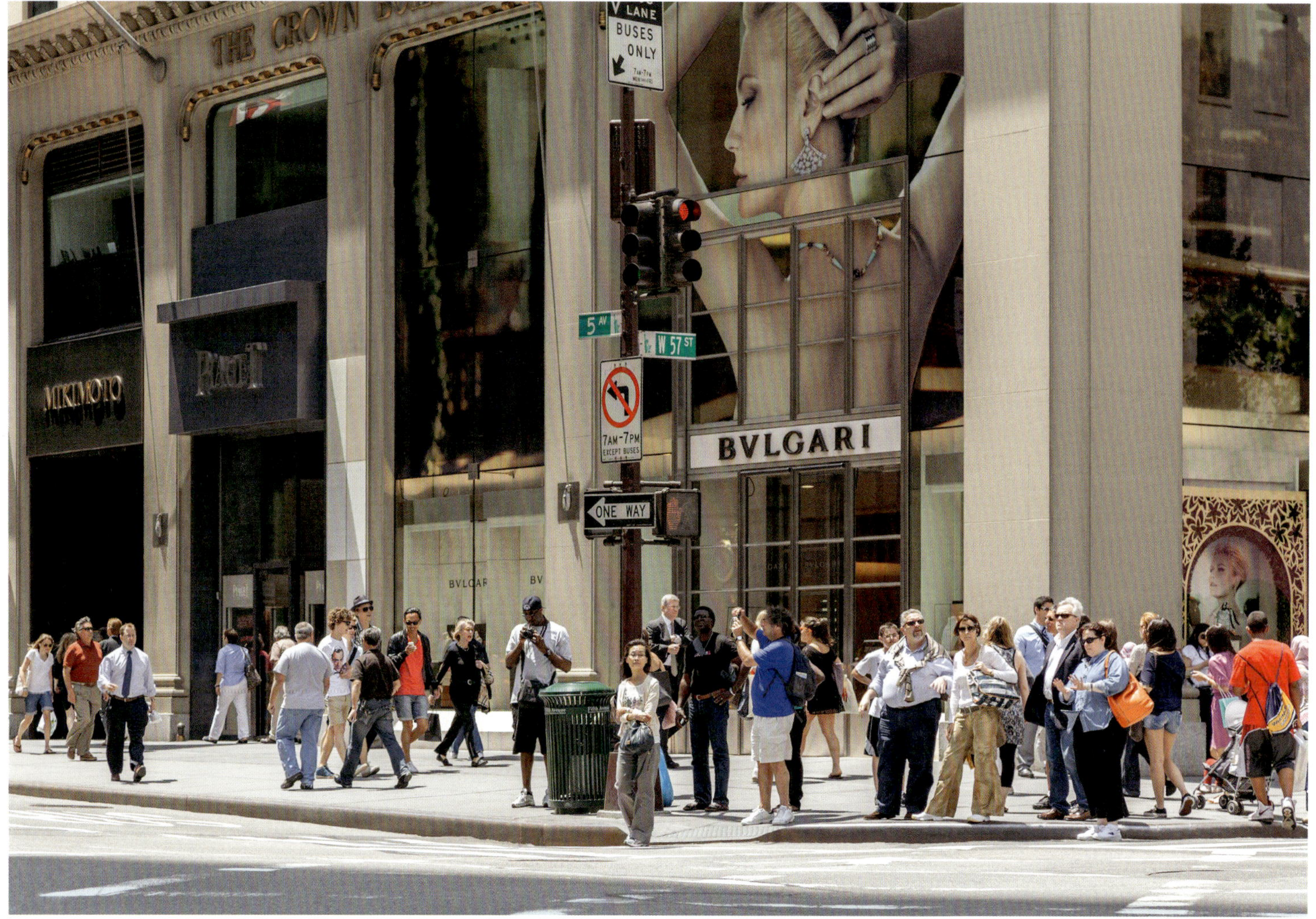

THE CROWN BUI
MIKIMOTO
PIAGET
5 AV
W 57 ST
BUSES ONLY
LANE
7AM-7PM EXCEPT BUSES
ONE WAY
BVLGARI

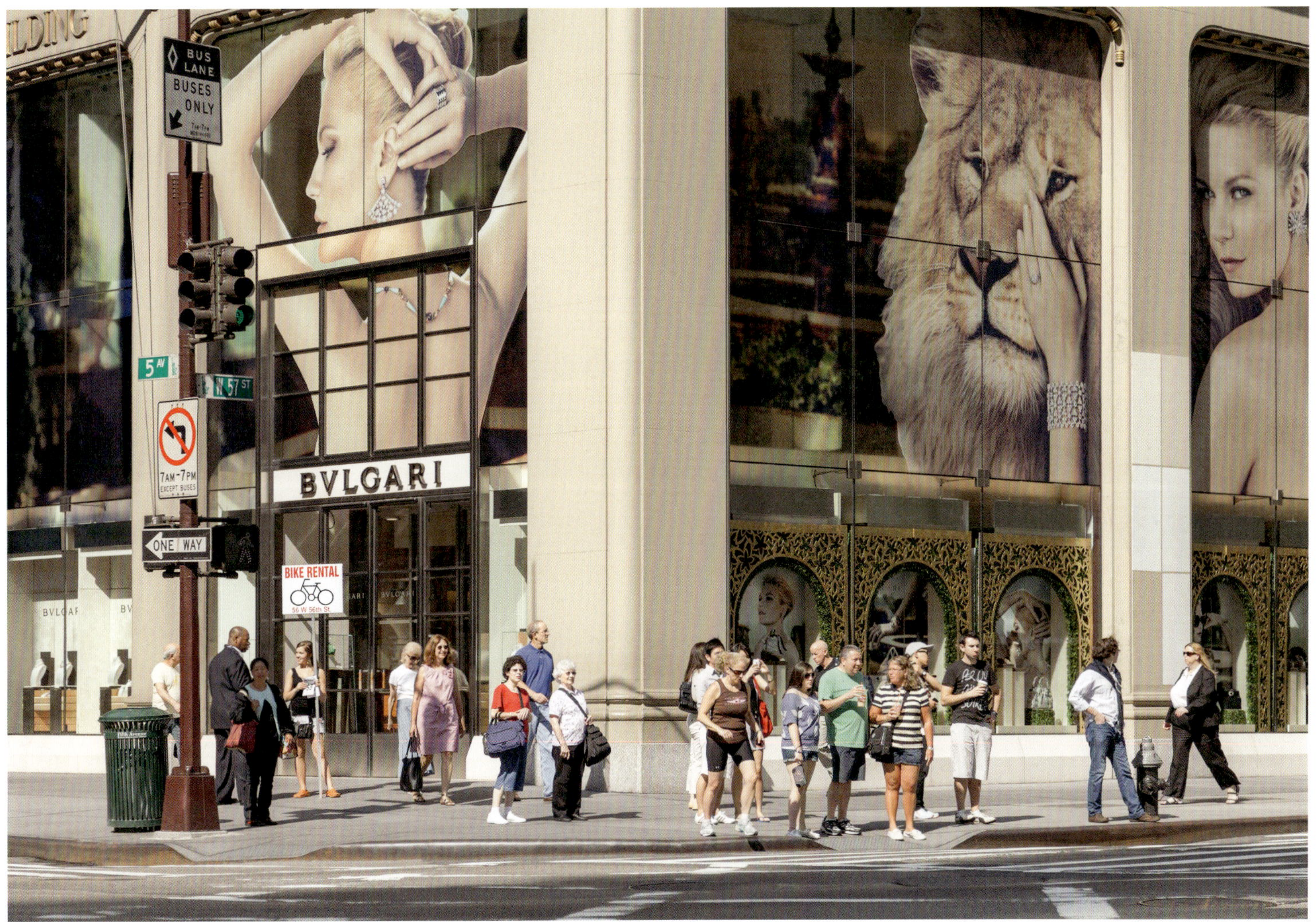
BUS
LANE
BUSES
ONLY
5 AV
W 57 ST
7AM-7PM
EXCEPT BUSES
ONE WAY
BIKE RENTAL
56 W 56th St
BVLGARI
BVLGARI

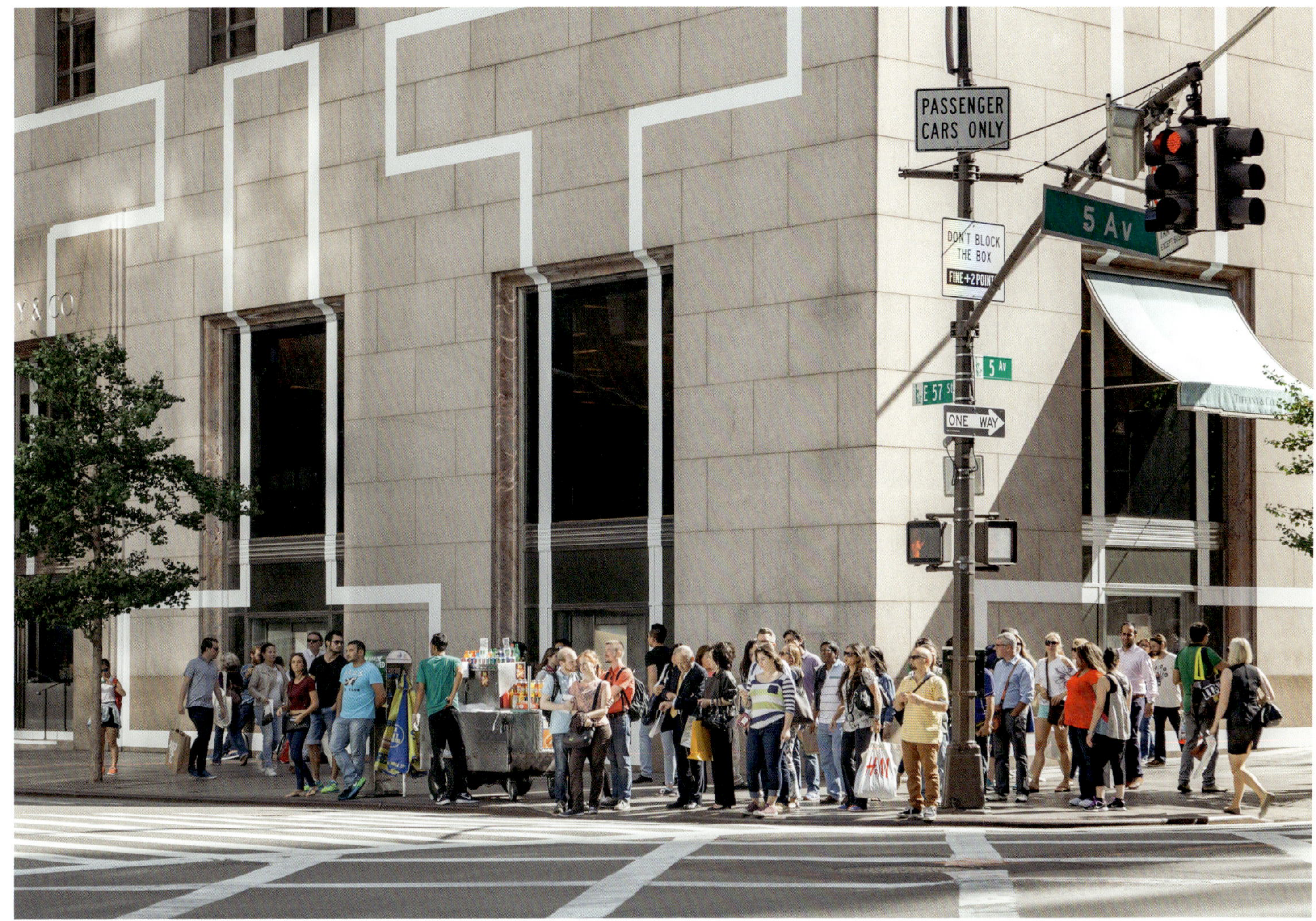

5th Avenue 71, 2014

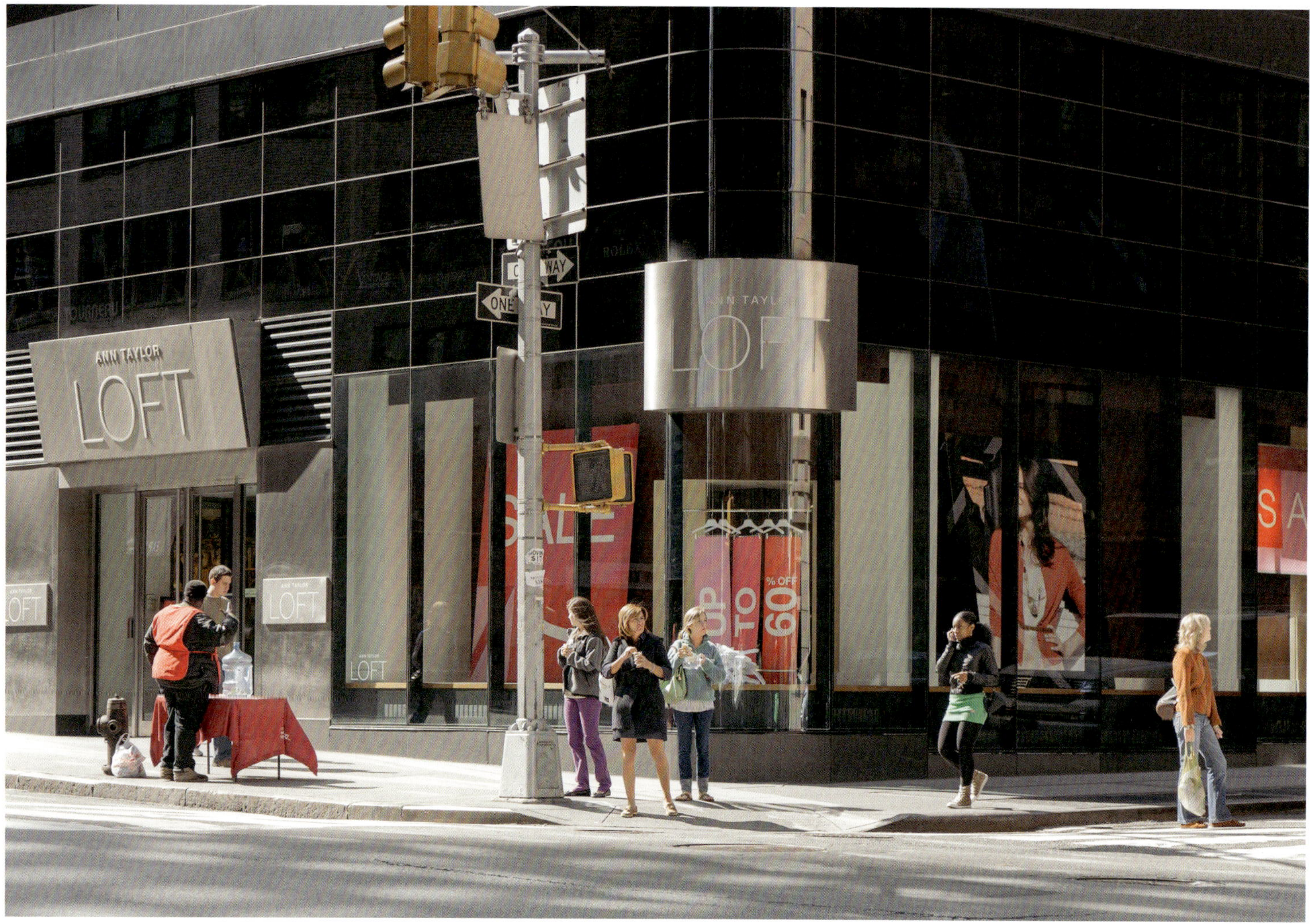

   Lexington Avenue 8, 2008

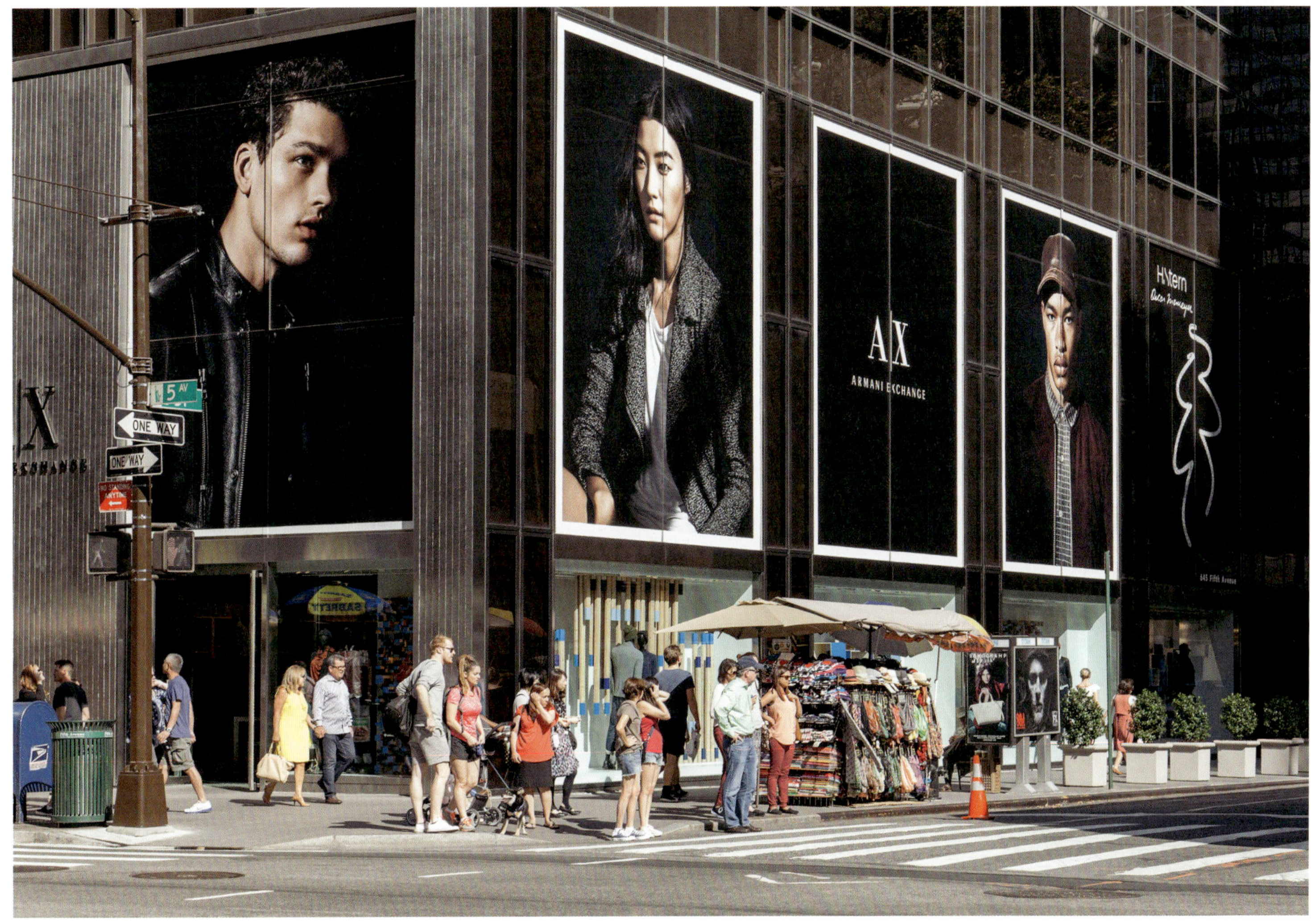5 AV
ONE WAY
ONE WAY
NO STANDING ANYTIME
AX
EXCHANGE
AX
ARMANI EXCHANGE
H Stern
645 Fifth Avenue
SABRETT

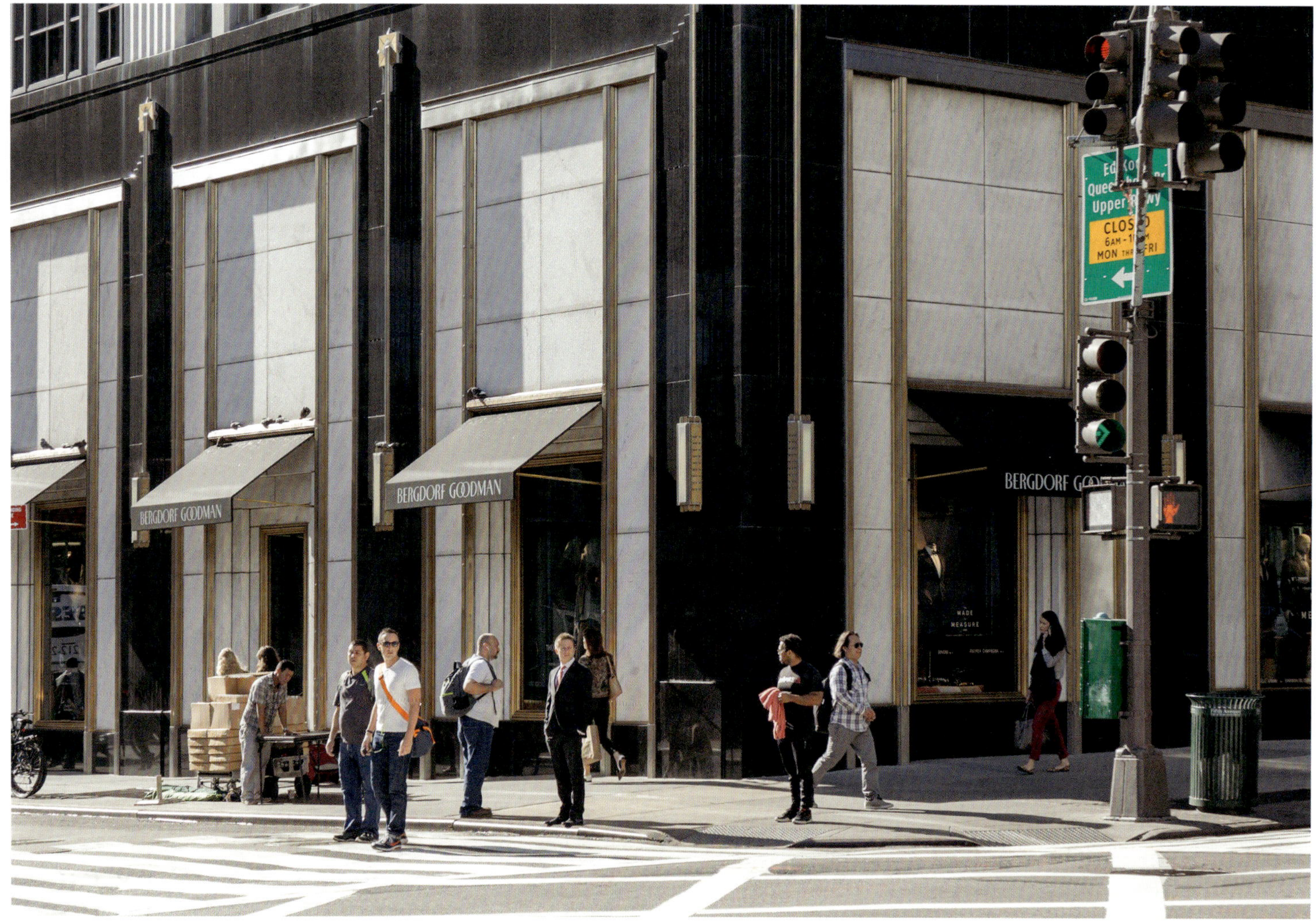

   58th Street 6, 2014

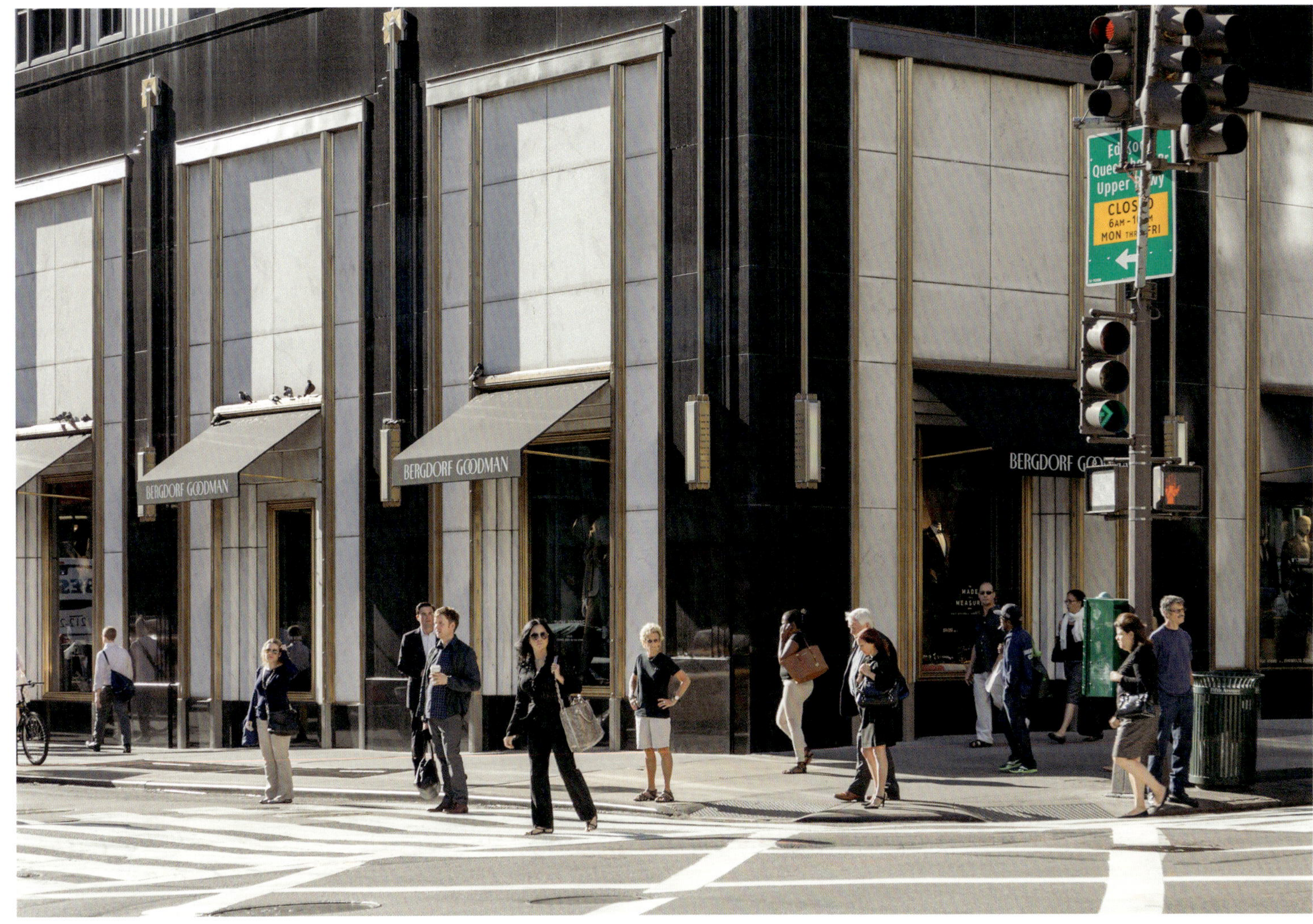

58th Street 4, 2014   41

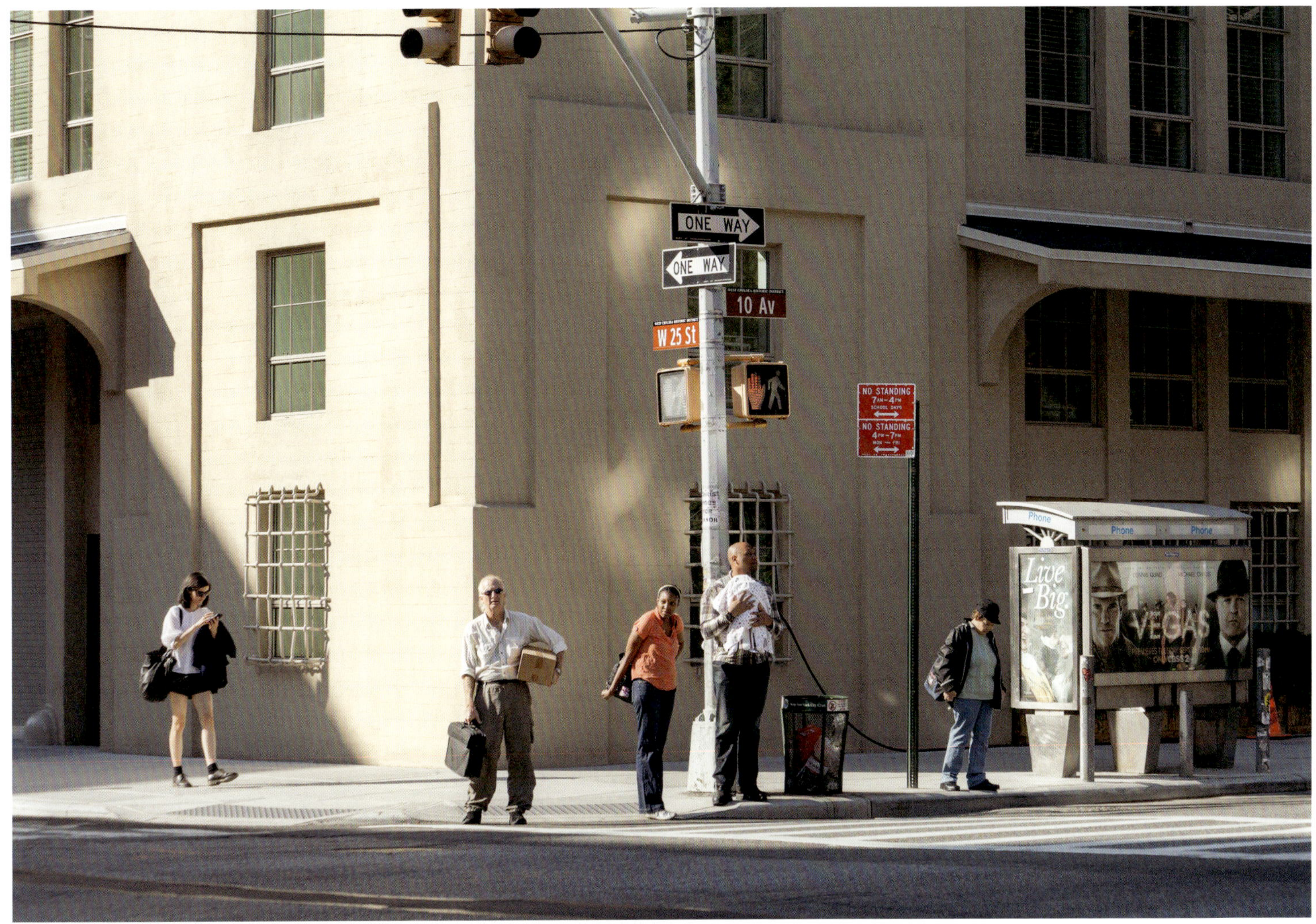

10th Avenue 9, 2012   43

Die Beobachtung der Schattenlänge eines vertikal ausgedehnten Objekts – eines Gnomons (griech. *Schattenzeiger*) – stellt den Beginn der Zeitmessung mittels Sonnenuhren dar. Manhattans Skyscraper wirken wie die Gnomone riesiger Sonnenuhren. Das Licht der Sonne bewegt sich um die Skyscraper herum und taucht die Straßen in einem festen Zeitrhythmus in Licht und Schatten. Szenen des Alltags sind zu bestimmten Zeiten hell erleuchtet und in gleißendes Licht getaucht – aber nur wenig später liegen sie schon wieder im dunklen Schatten. Es entstehen Bilder, die eine geradezu unwirkliche Kraft besitzen und uns die Schönheit alltäglicher Situationen deutlich machen. Die urbane Architektur wird zu einer Bühne, auf der die Protagonisten agieren. Das Licht in Manhattan ist hell und klar und fast wirkt es, als ob es nur dafür geschaffen wurde, die ganze Szenerie dieser riesigen Bühne auf natürliche Weise perfekt auszuleuchten. Es ist ein Licht, das moduliert, kontrastreich und kraftvoll ist – kühle Morgenstunden, strahlende Mittagssonne, grelles Licht und dunkle Schatten im Rhythmus des stetigen Laufs der Sonne.

The observation of the shadow length of a vertically extended object—a gnomon (Greek for *shadow hand*)—represents the beginning of time measurement using sundials. Manhattan's skyscrapers act like the gnomons of giant sundials. The light of the sun moves around them and immerses the streets in light and shadow in a fixed rhythm of time. Everyday scenes are brightly lit at certain times and bathed in a glistening light—but just a short time later, they lie in dark shade once again. Pictures are created that possess an almost unreal power, and make the beauty of seemingly ordinary situations clear to us. Urban architecture becomes a stage on which the protagonists act. The light in Manhattan is bright and clear and it seems almost as if it was only created to perfectly illuminate the whole scenery of this huge stage in a natural way. It is a light that is modulated, rich in contrasts, and powerful: cool morning hours, glittering midday sun, bright light and dark shadows in the rhythm of the steady course of the sun.

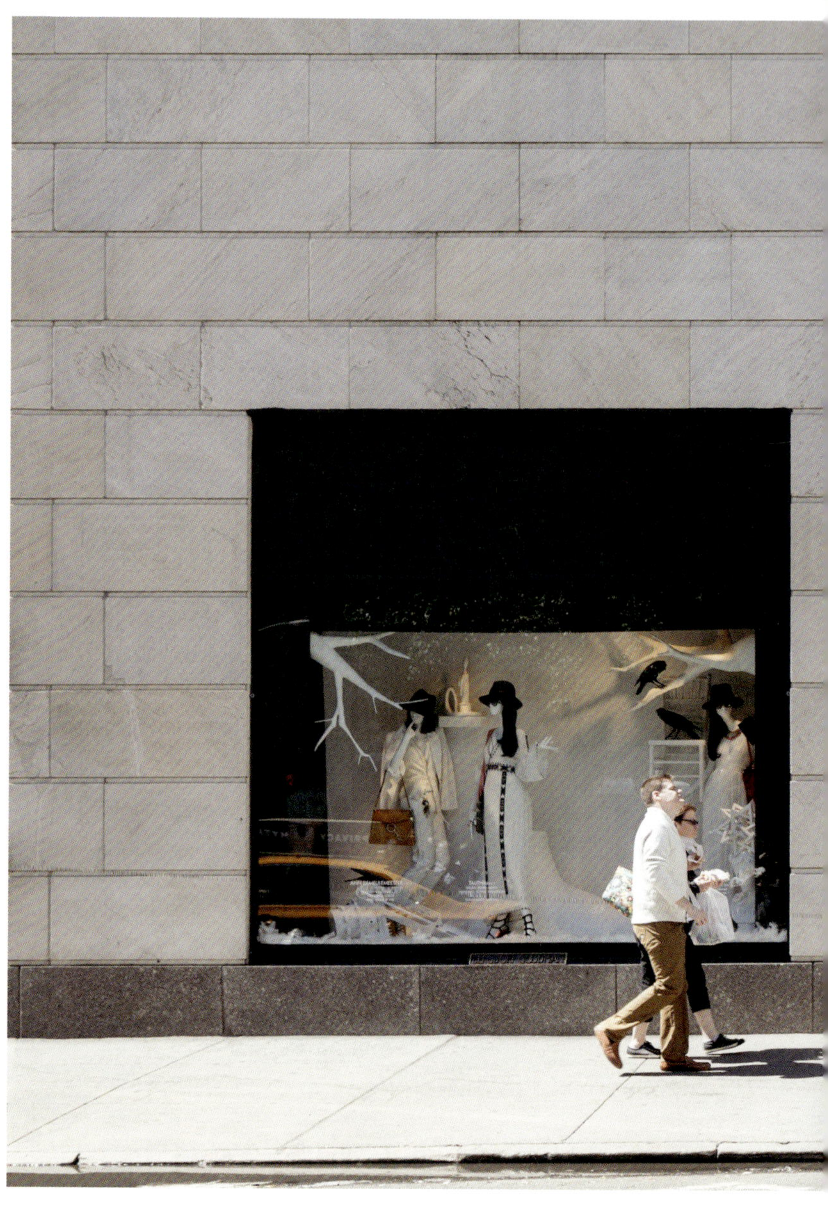

46   59th Street 1, 2016

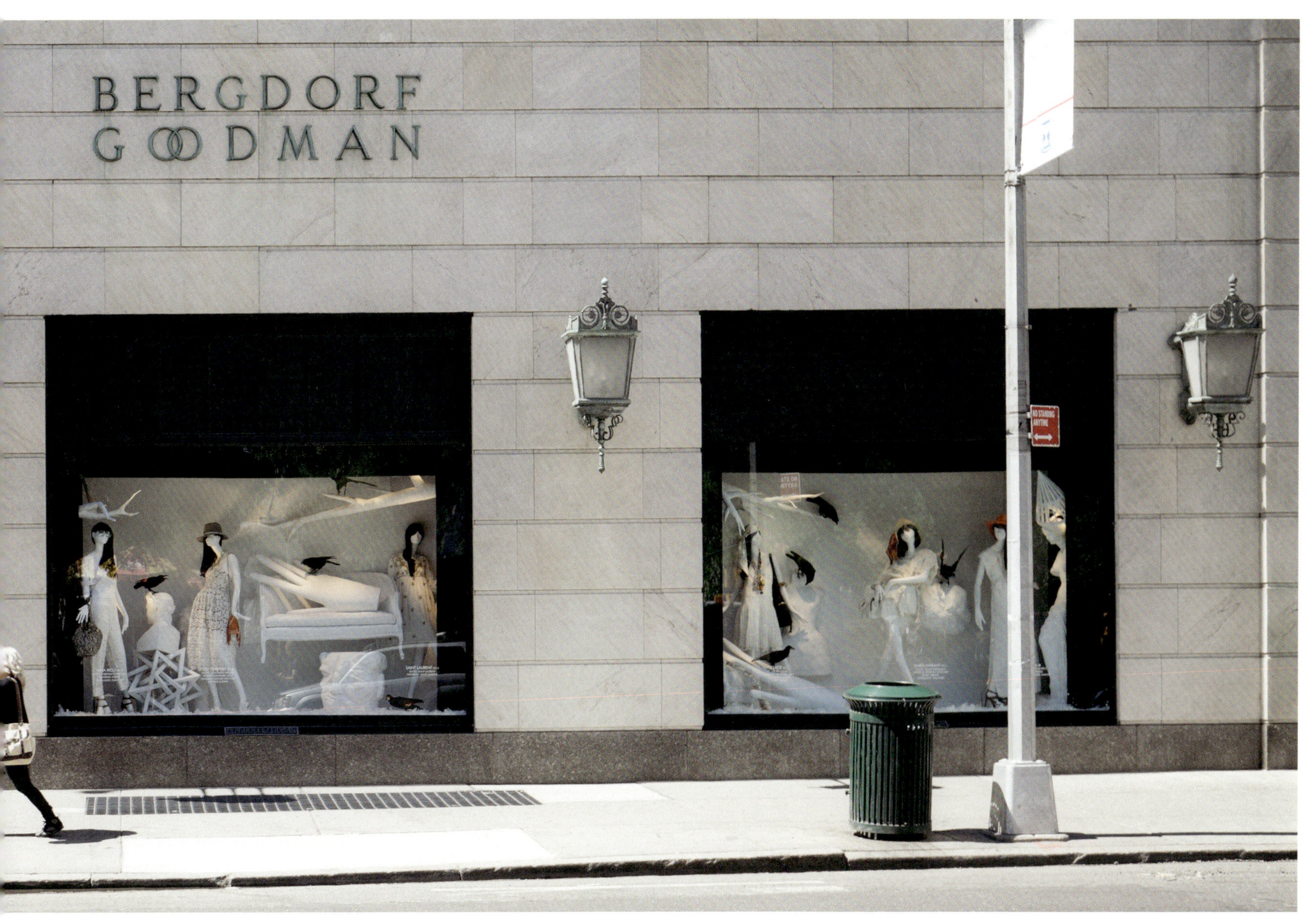

BERGDORF
GOODMAN

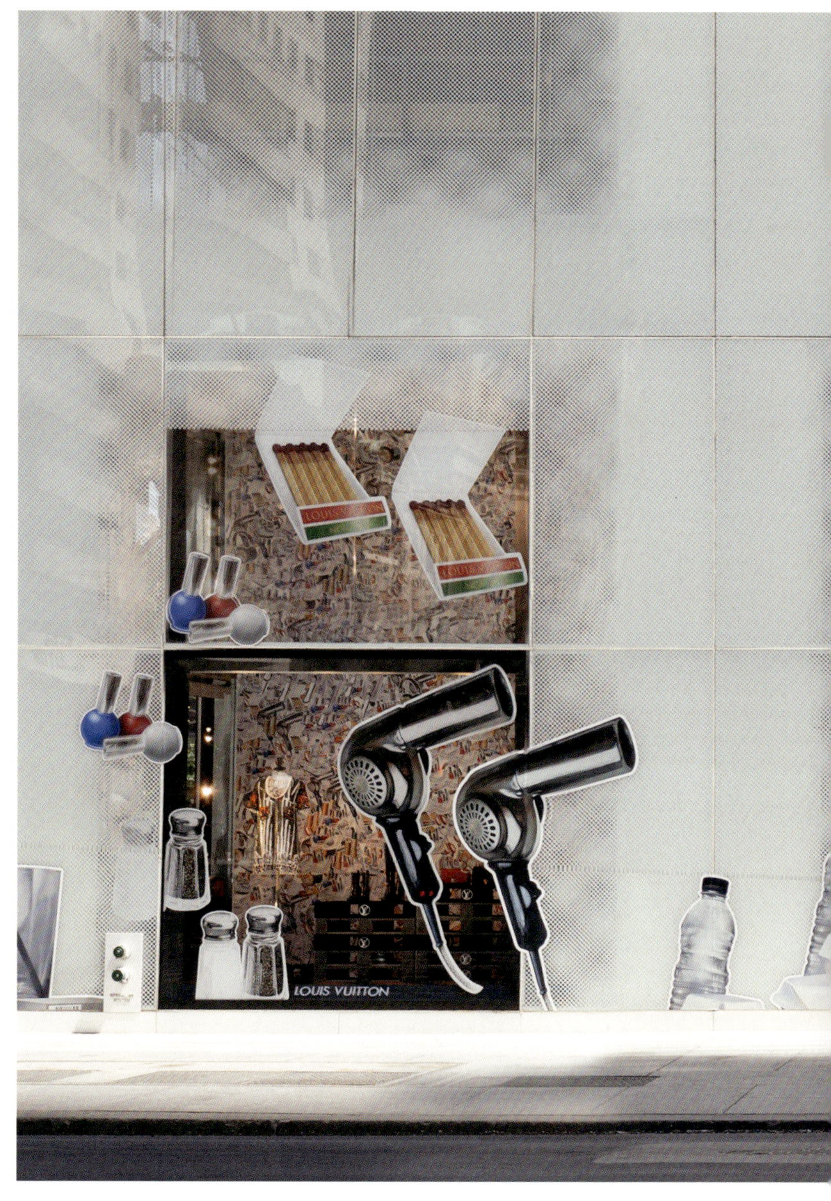

LOUIS VUITTON

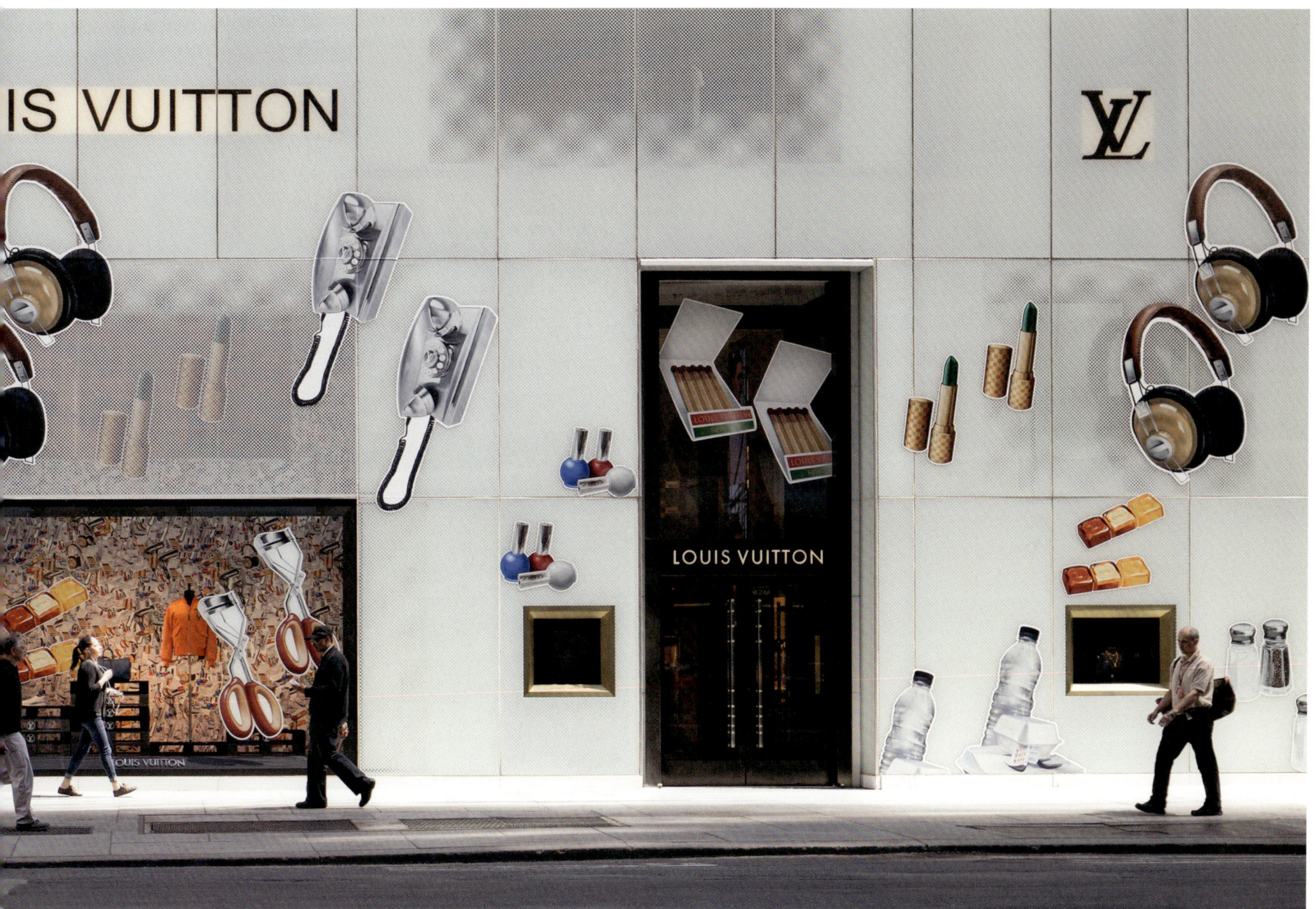

IS VUITTON
LV
LOUIS VUITTON
LOUIS VUITTON

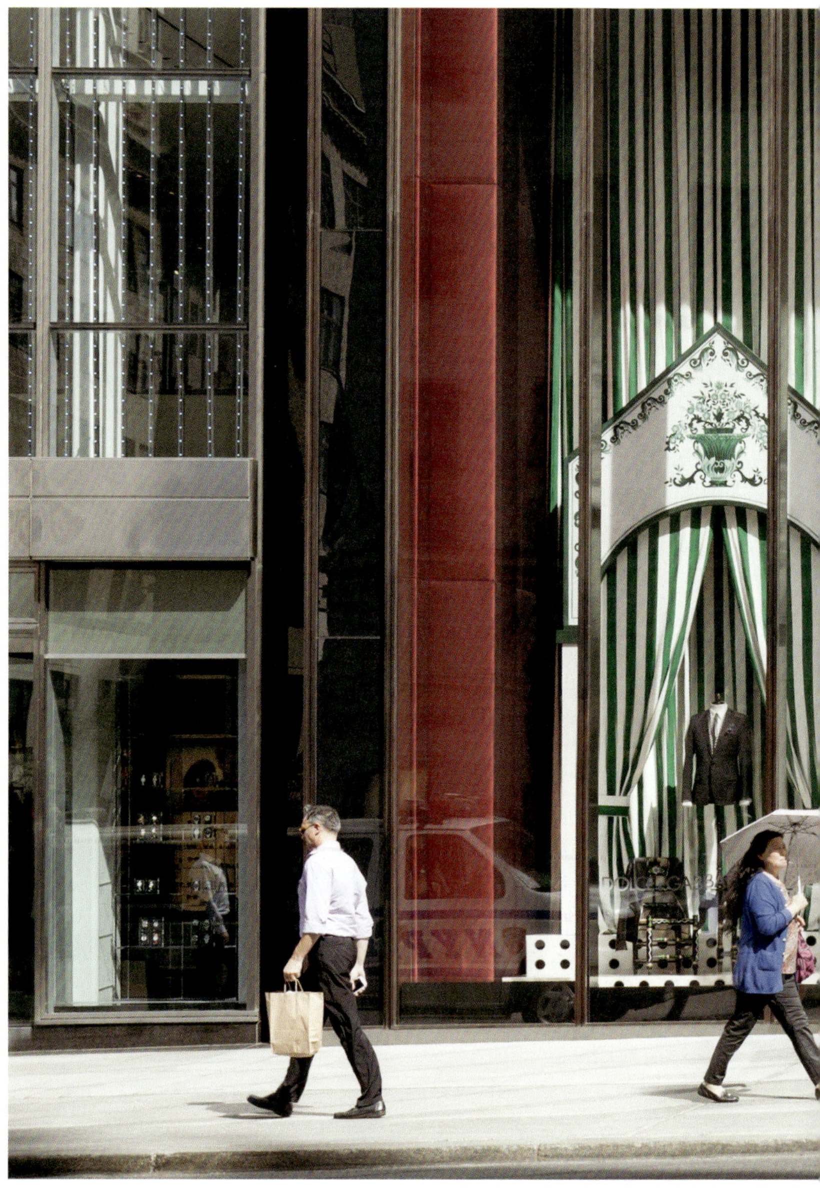

    5th Avenue 26, 2016

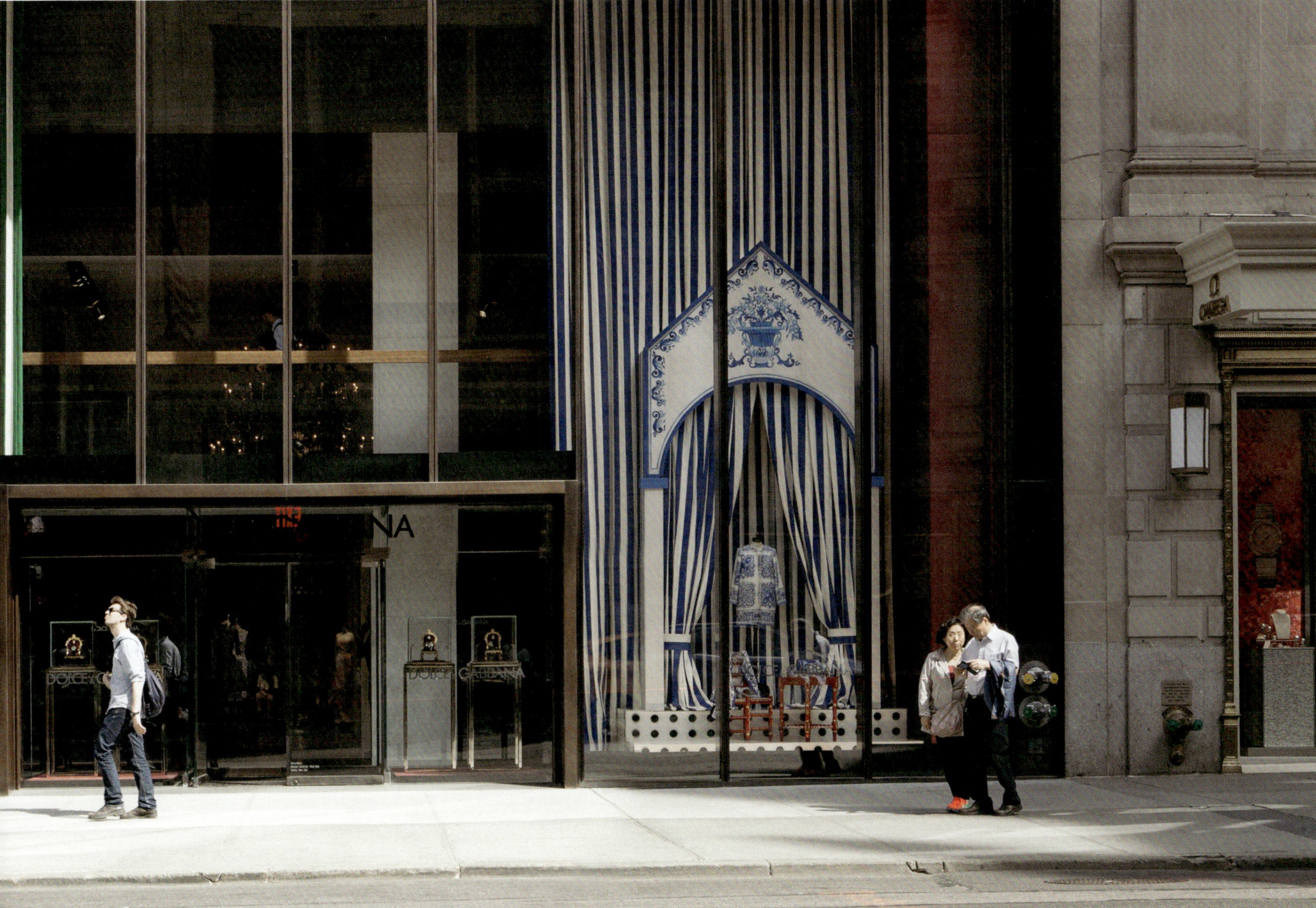

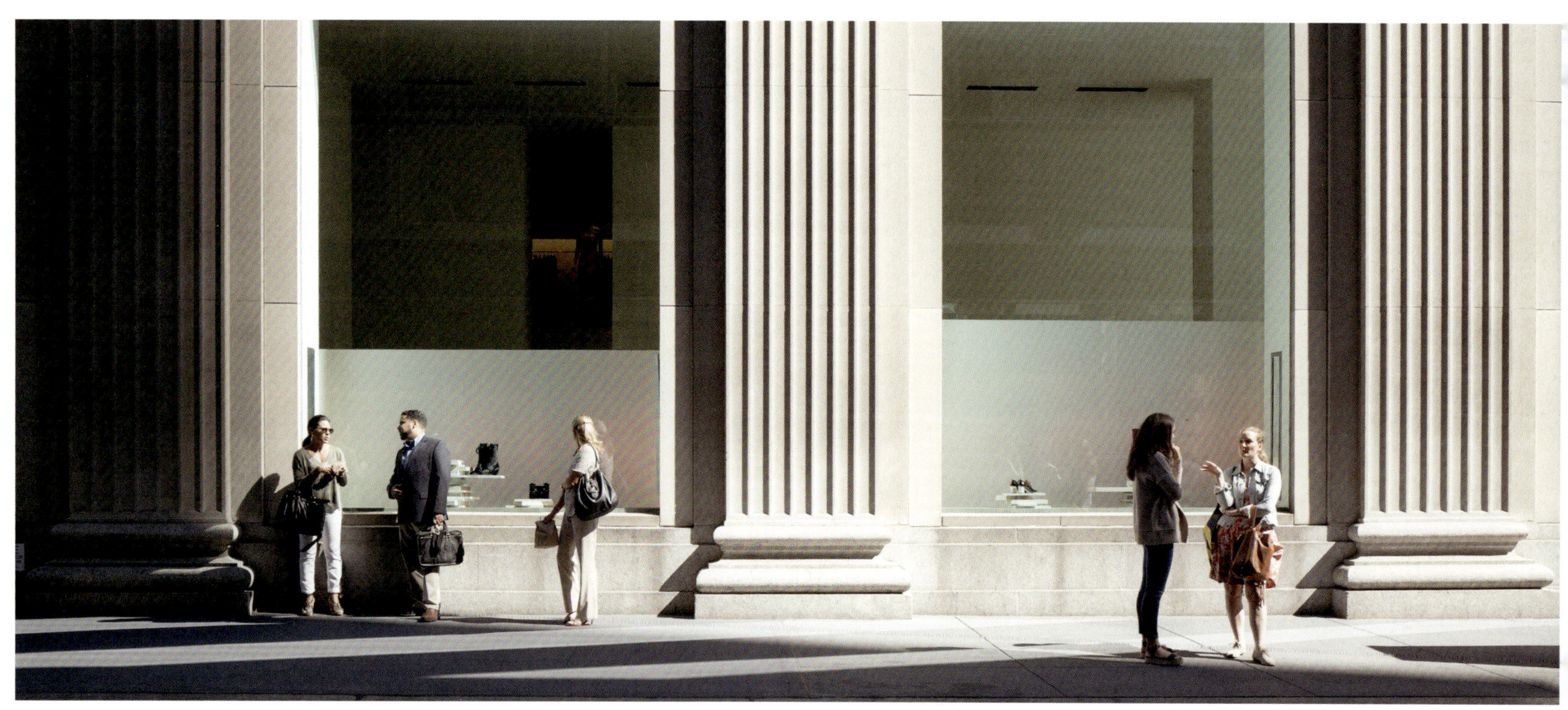

52   60th Street 1, 2016

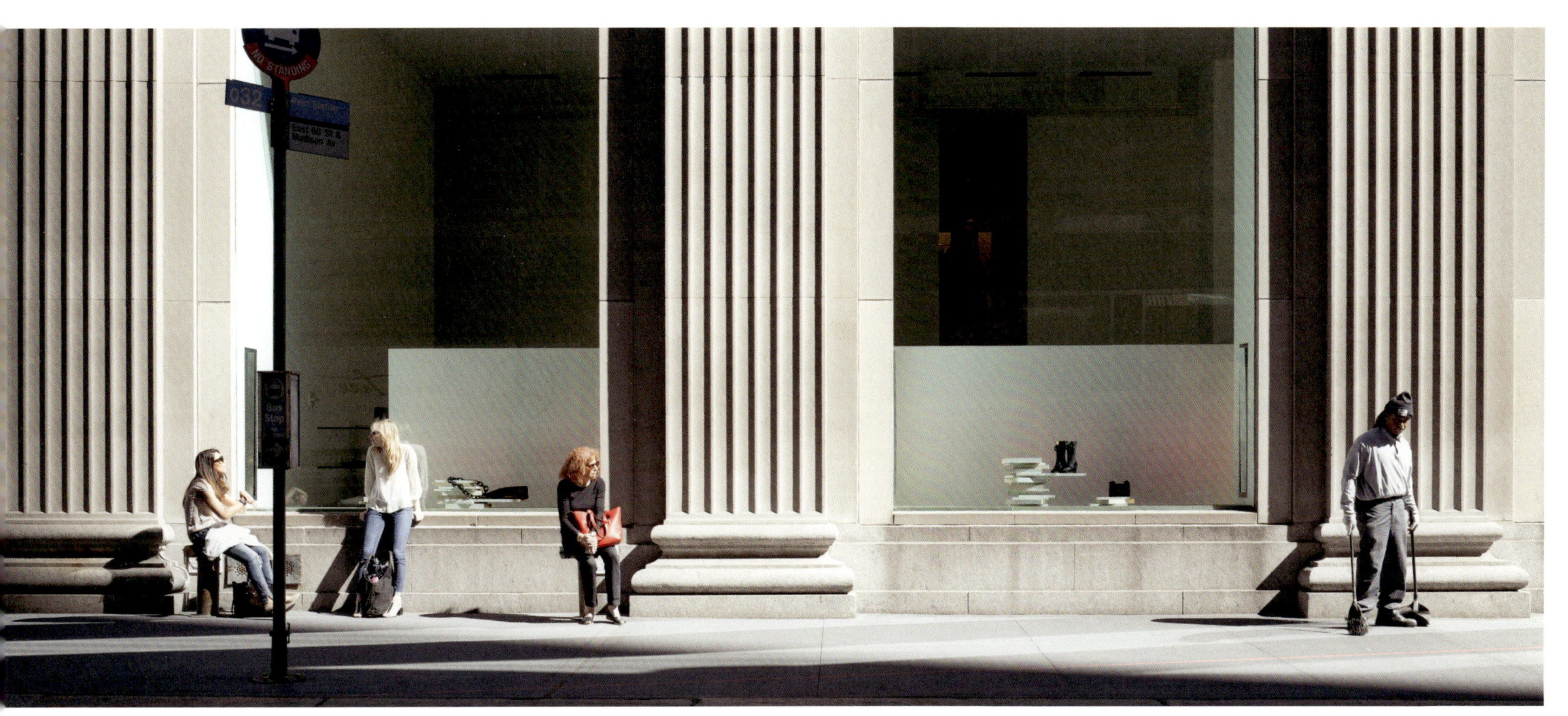

60th Street 2, 2016

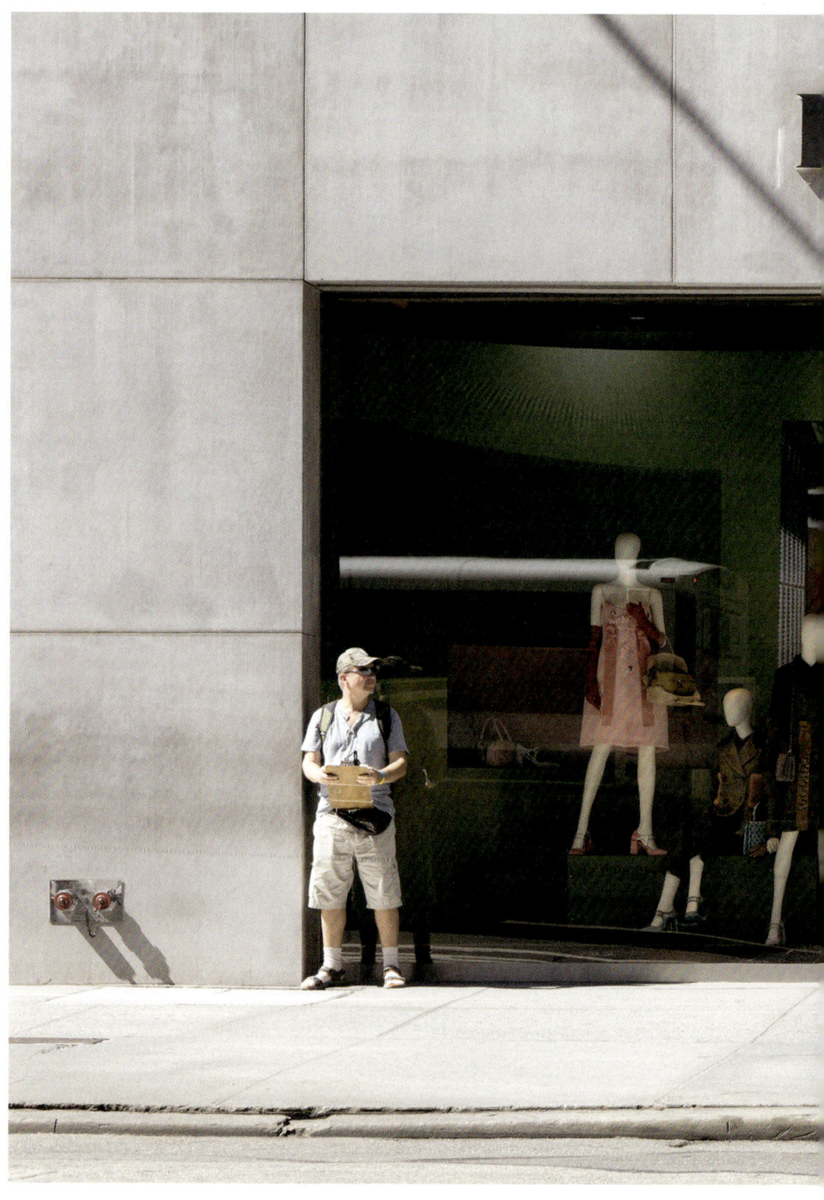

54   42nd Street 3, 2018

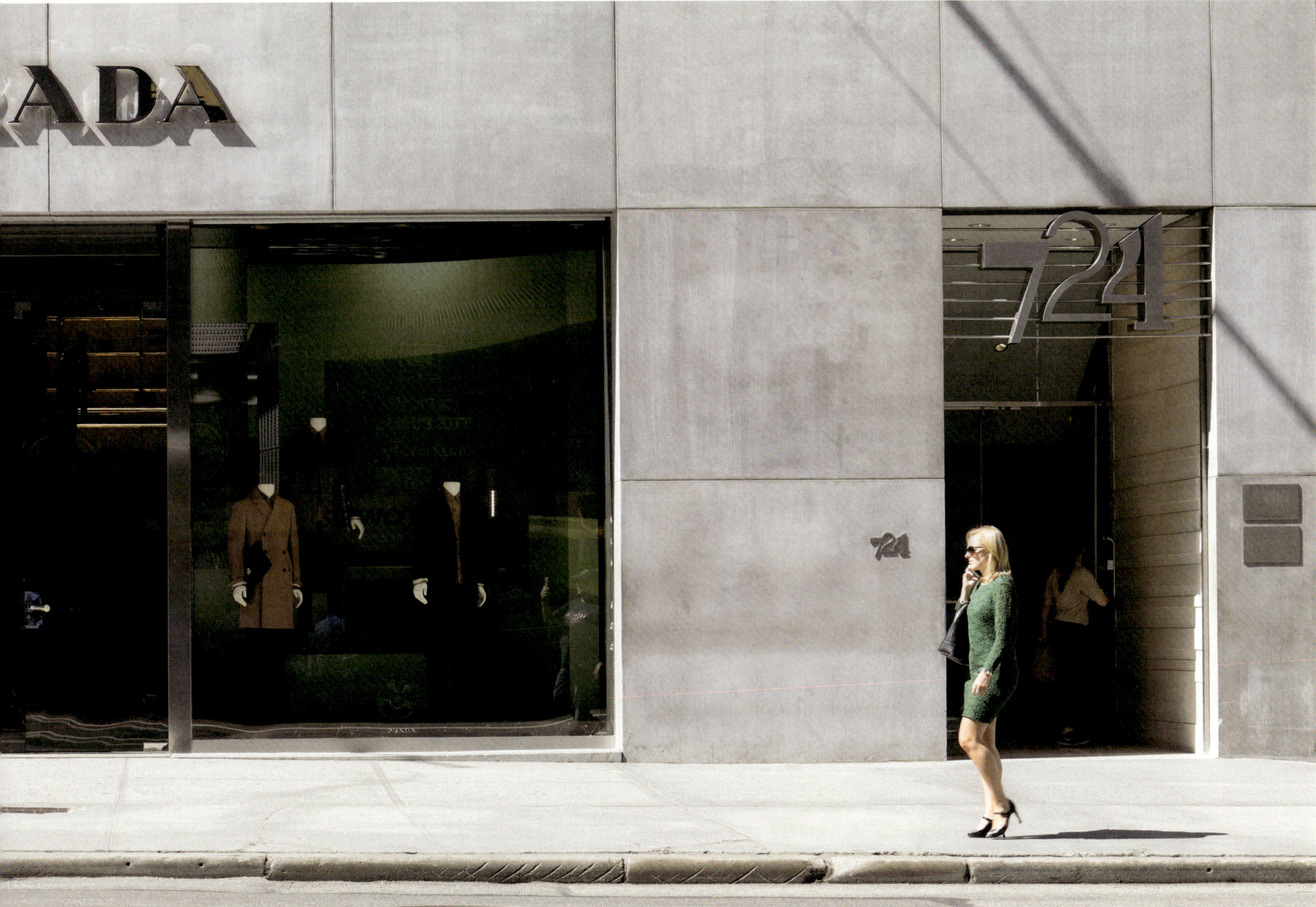

ADA
721
721

     5th Street 44, 2018

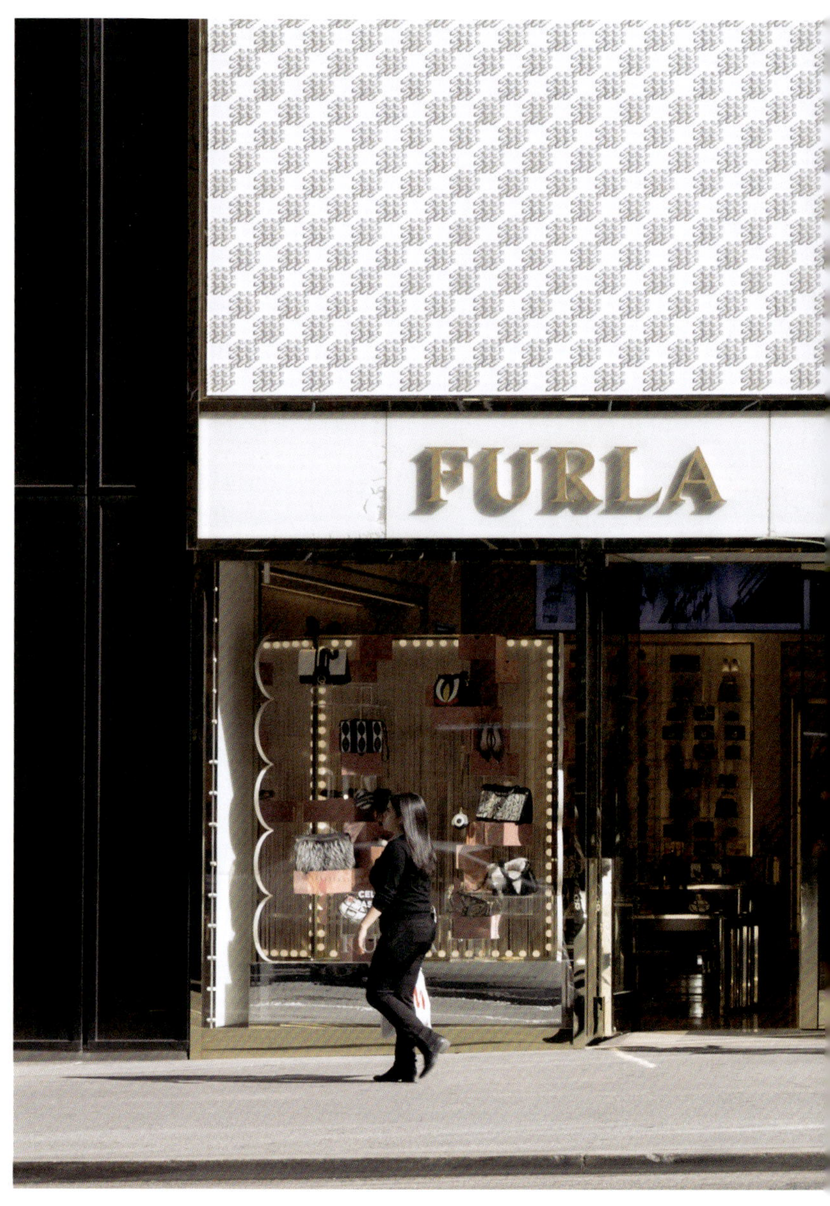

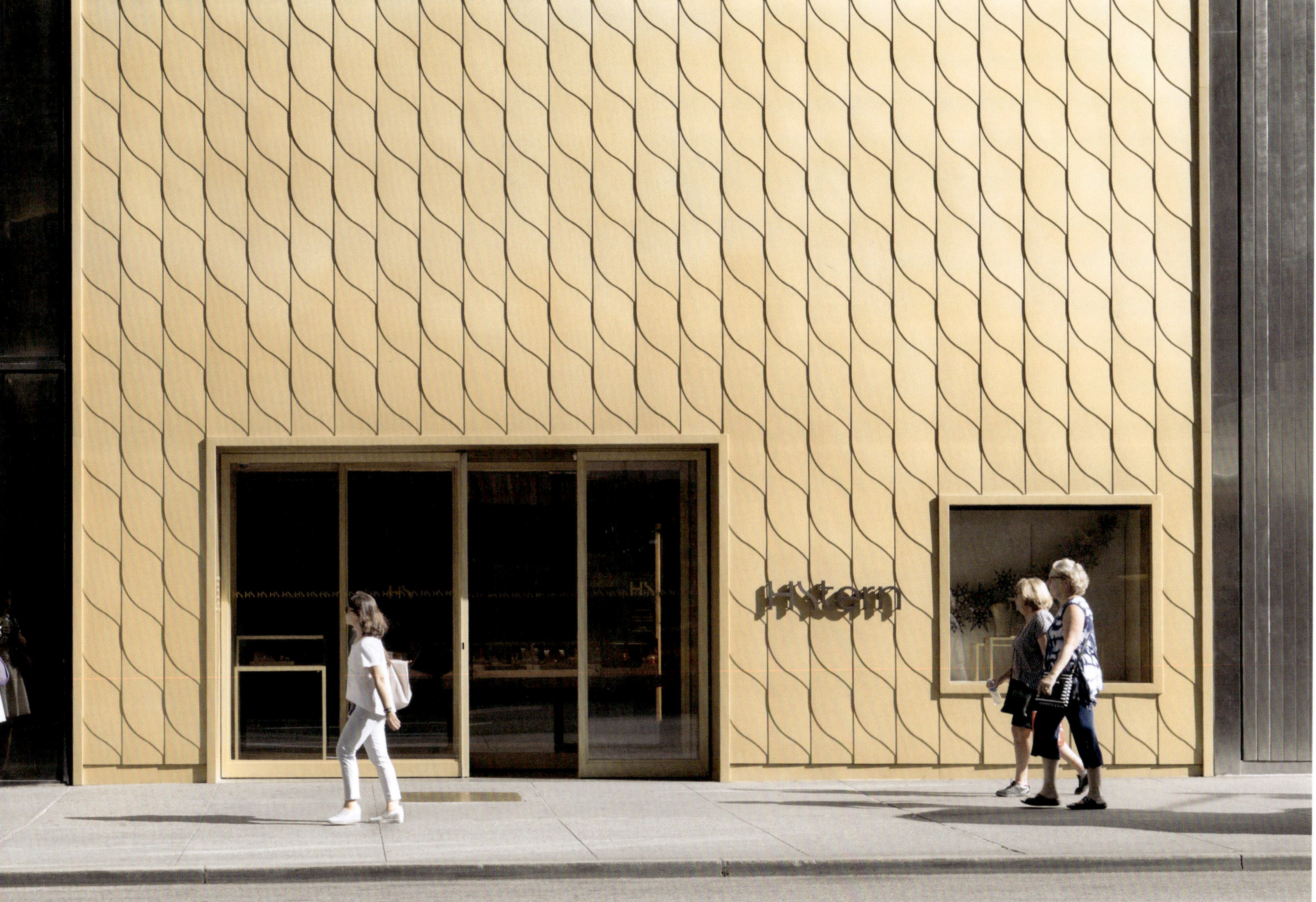

H.Stern

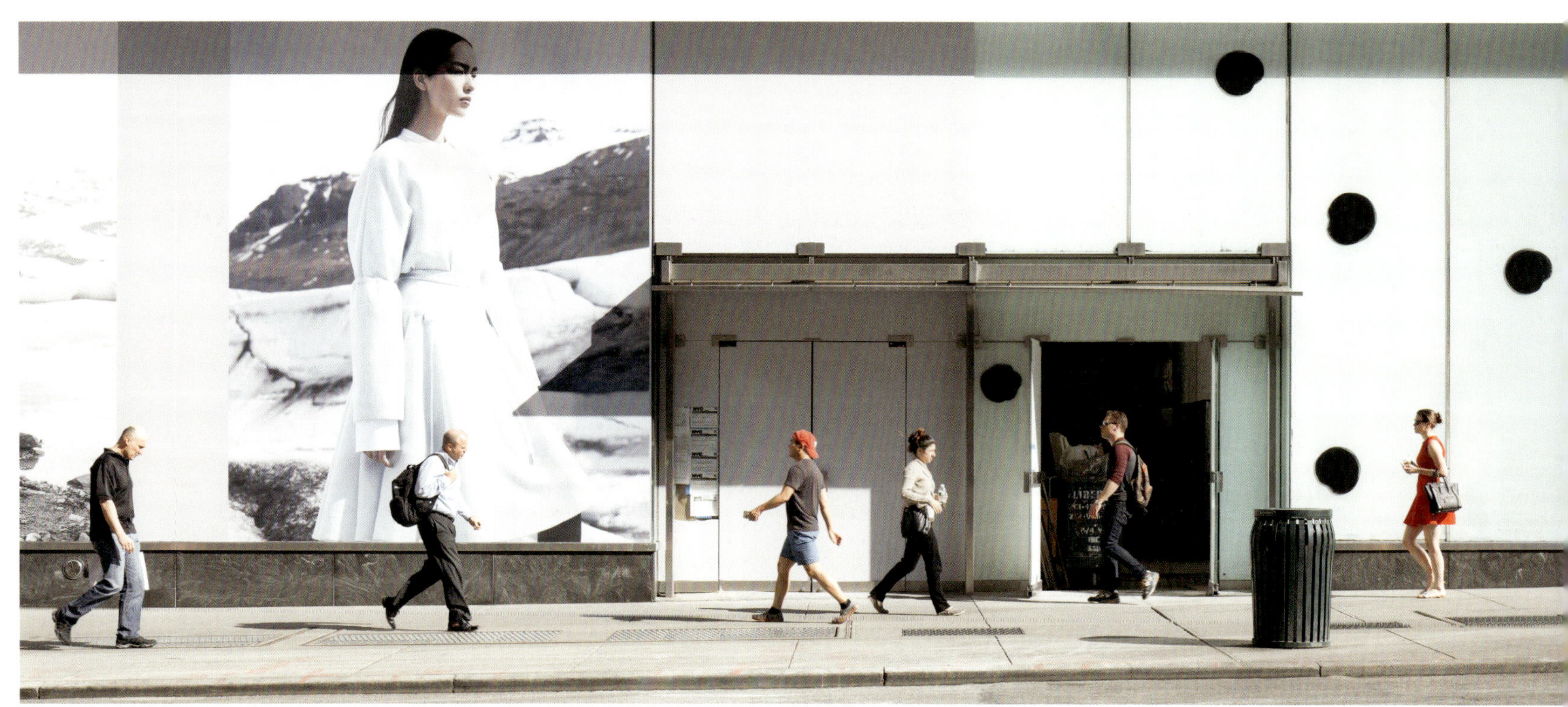

58   5th Avenue 34, 2016

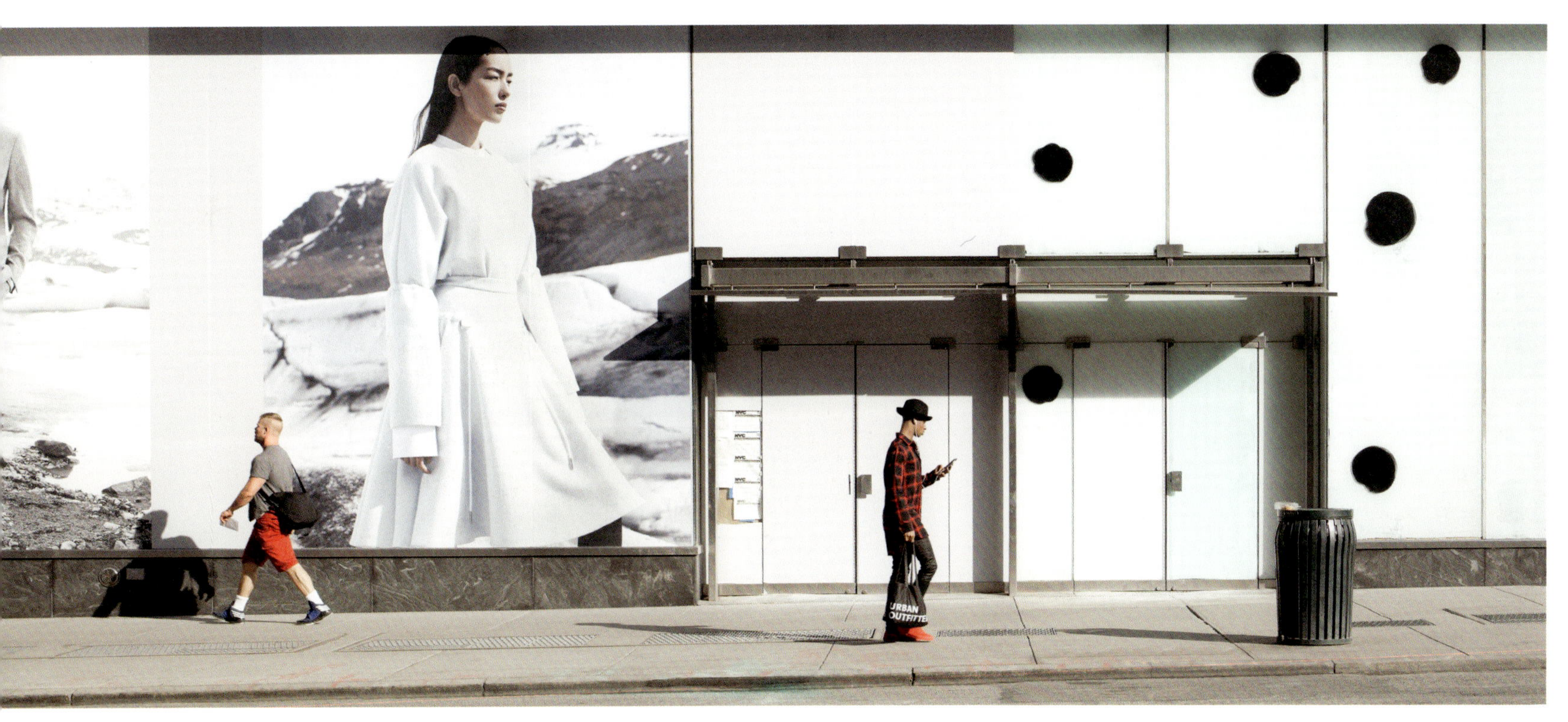

5th Avenue 35, 2016

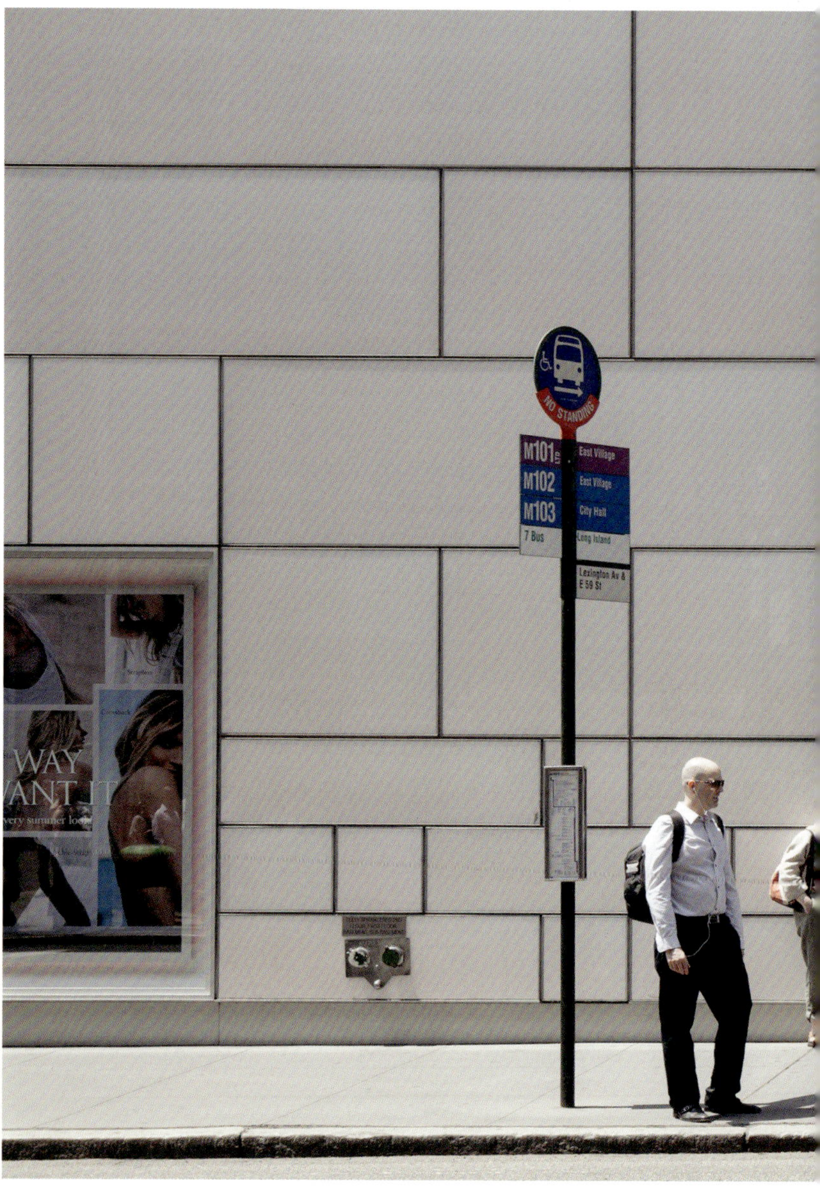

NO STANDING
M101 LTD East Village
M102 East Village
M103 City Hall
7 Bus Long Island
Lexington Av &
E 59 St

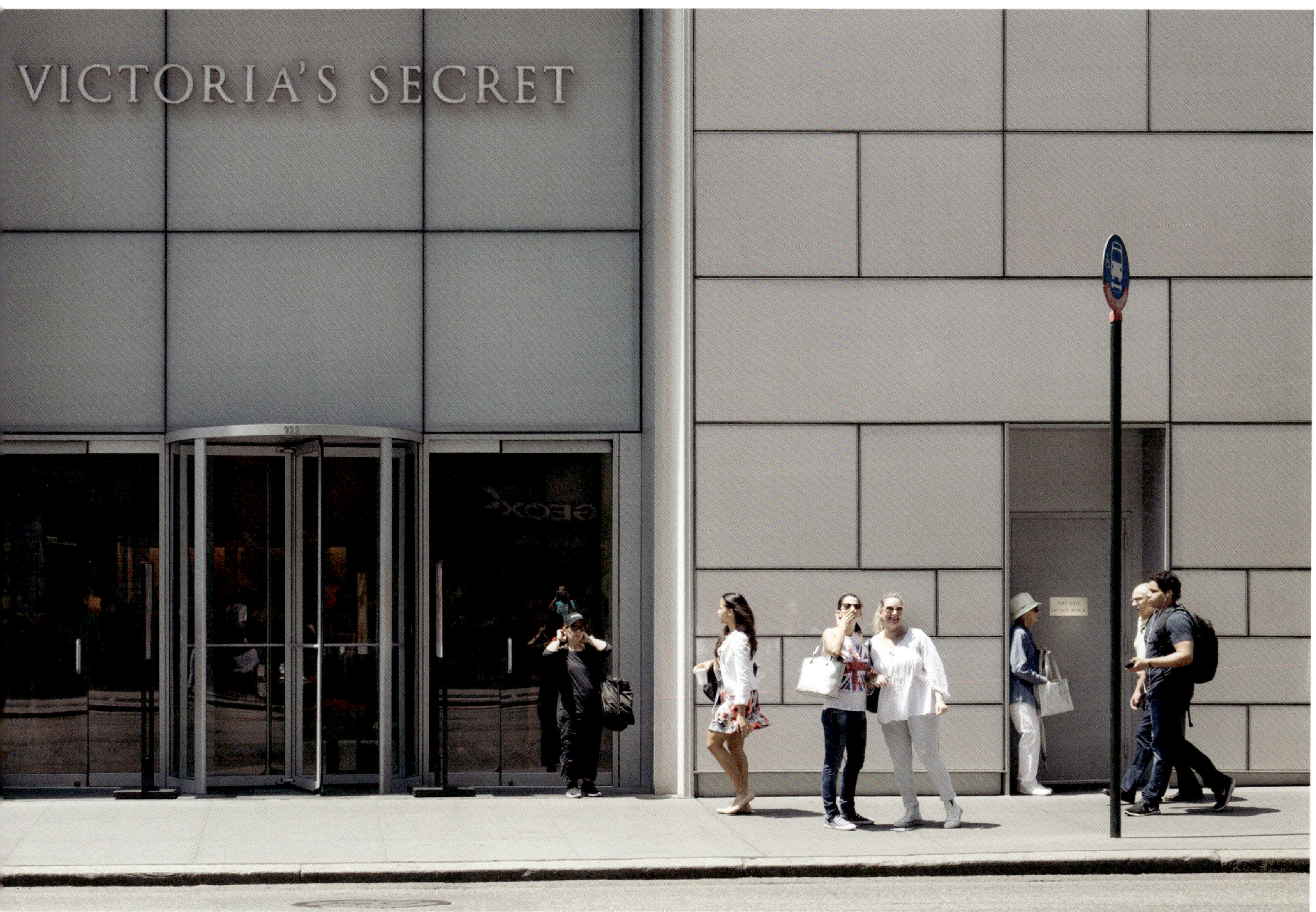

VICTORIA'S SECRET
GEOX

    42nd Street 1, 2016

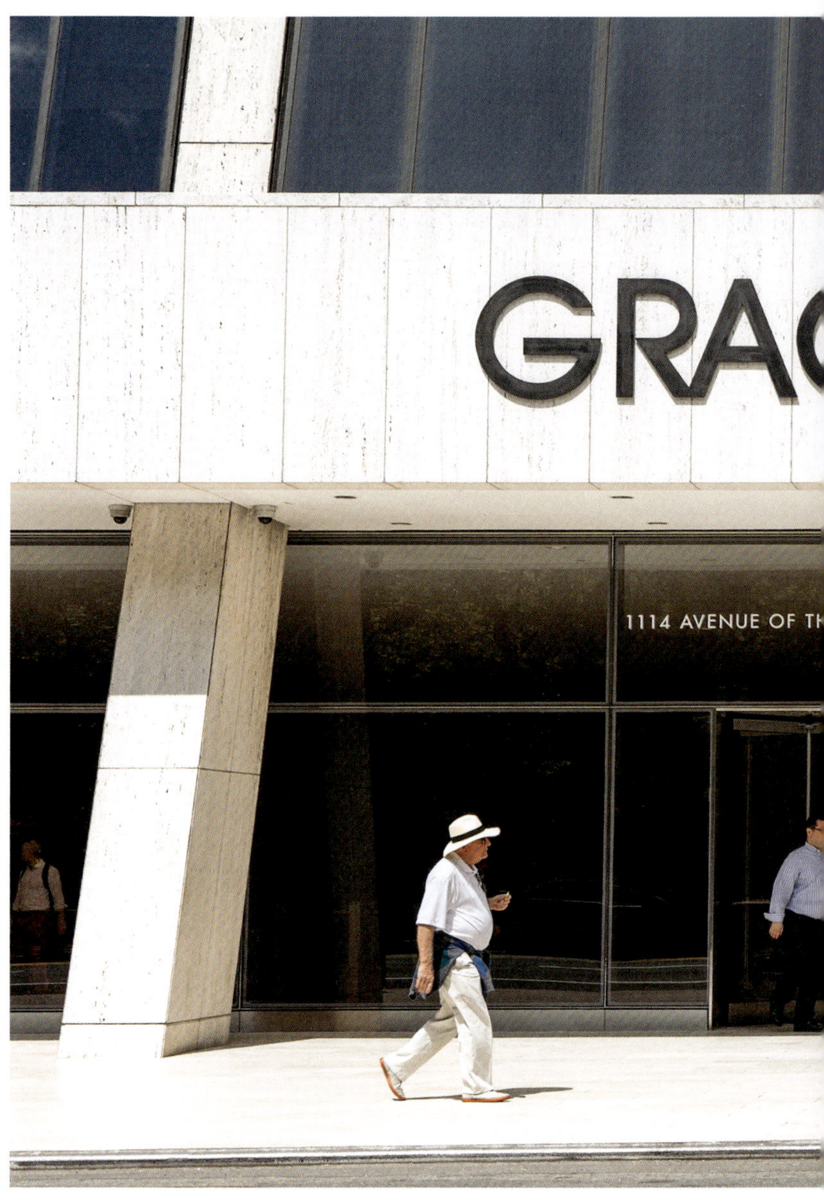

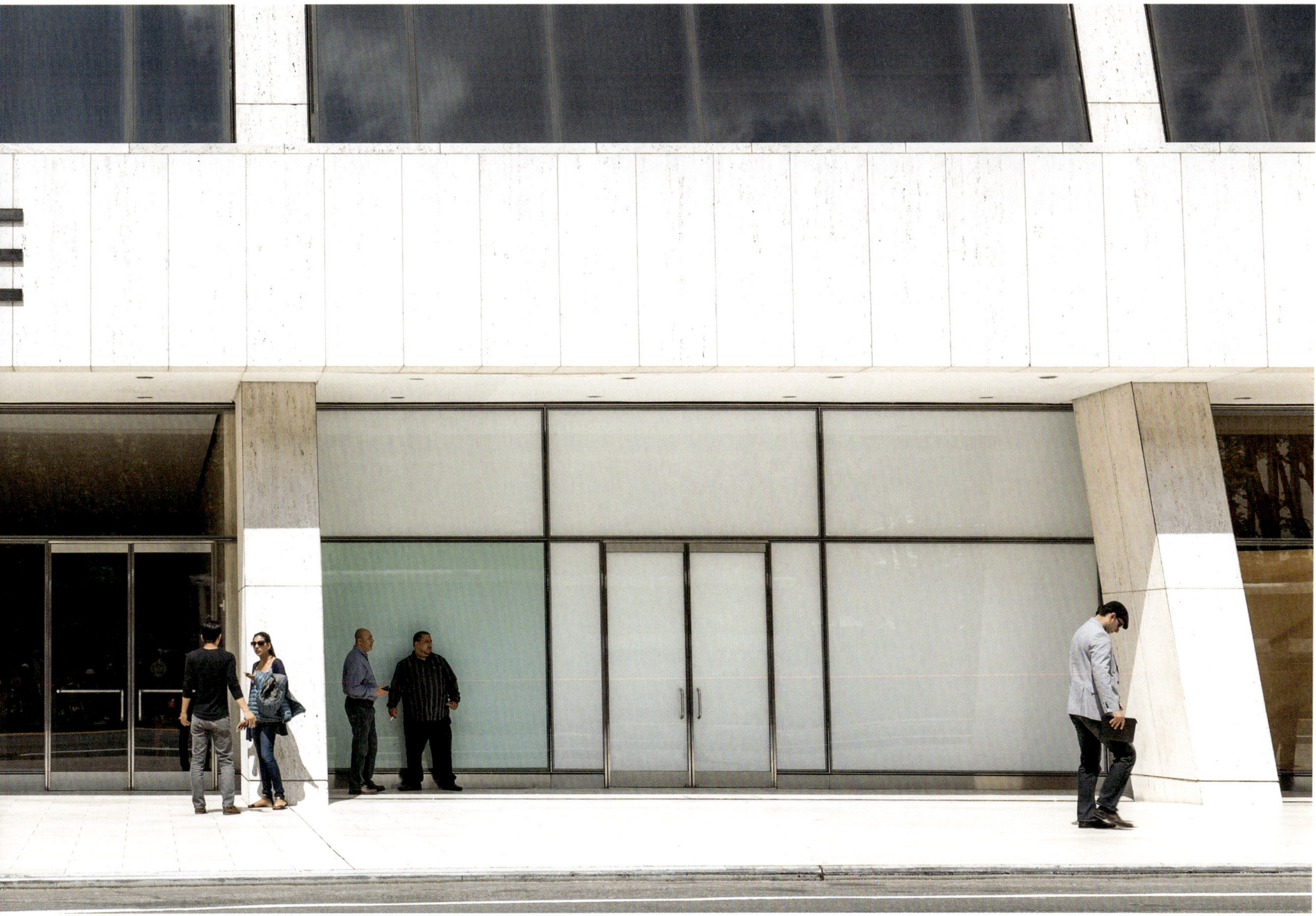

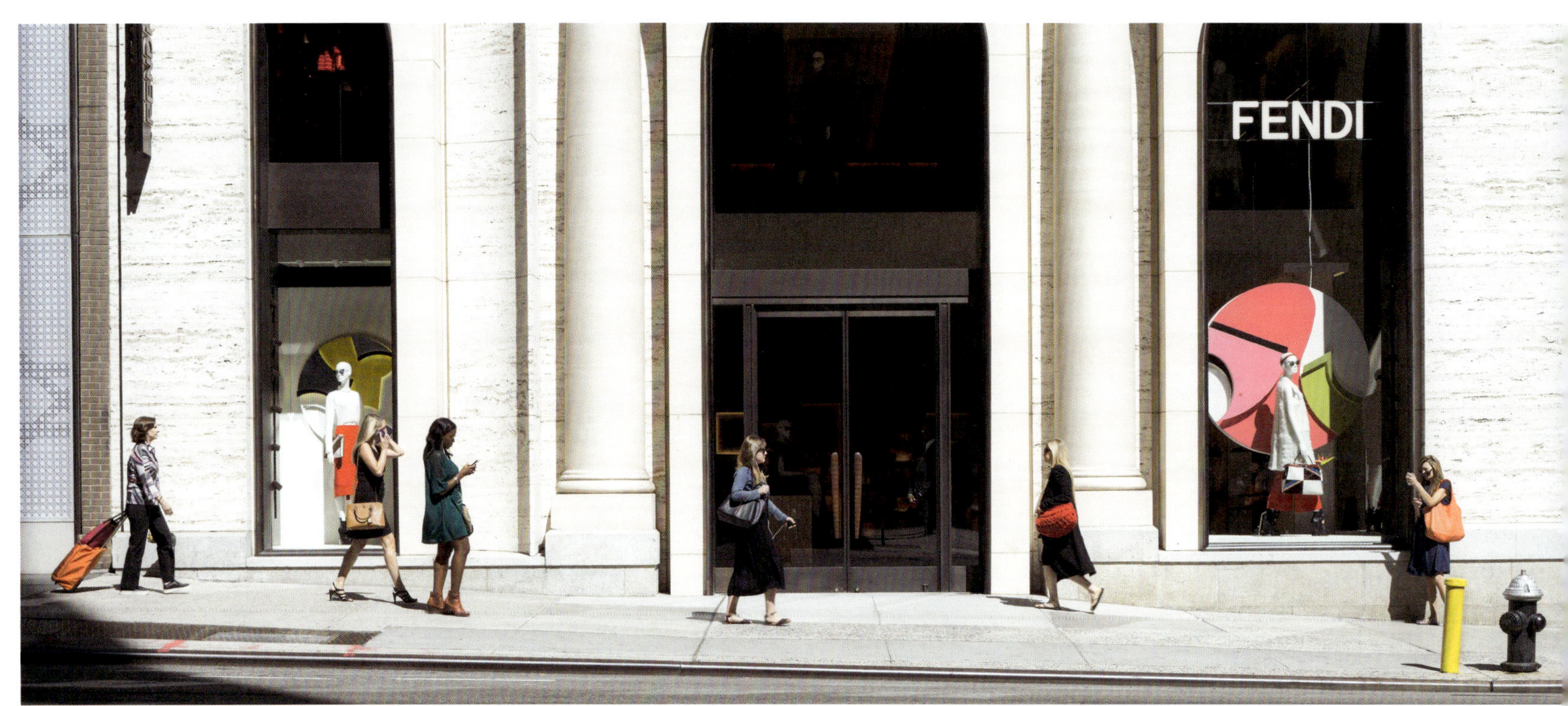

64   57th Street 2, 2018

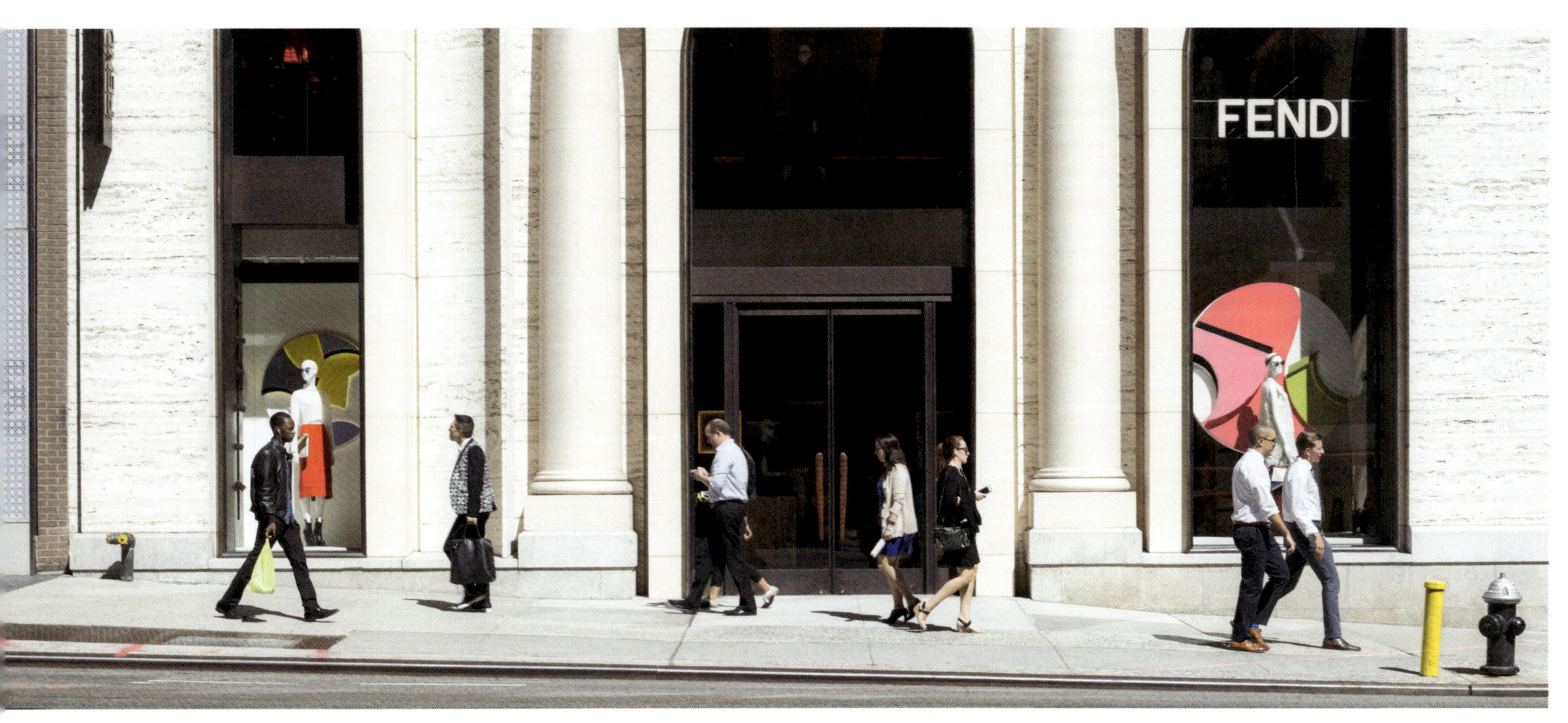

57th Street 3, 2018

    5th Avenue 39, 2018

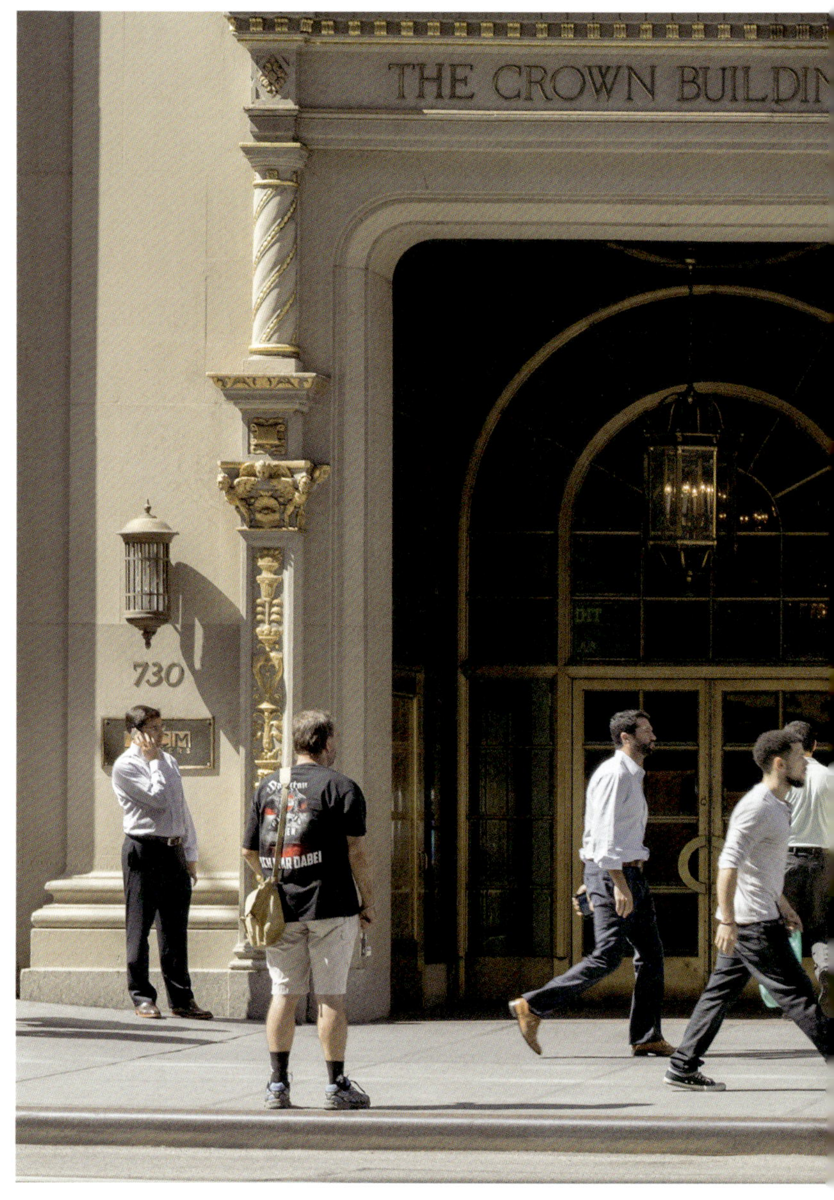

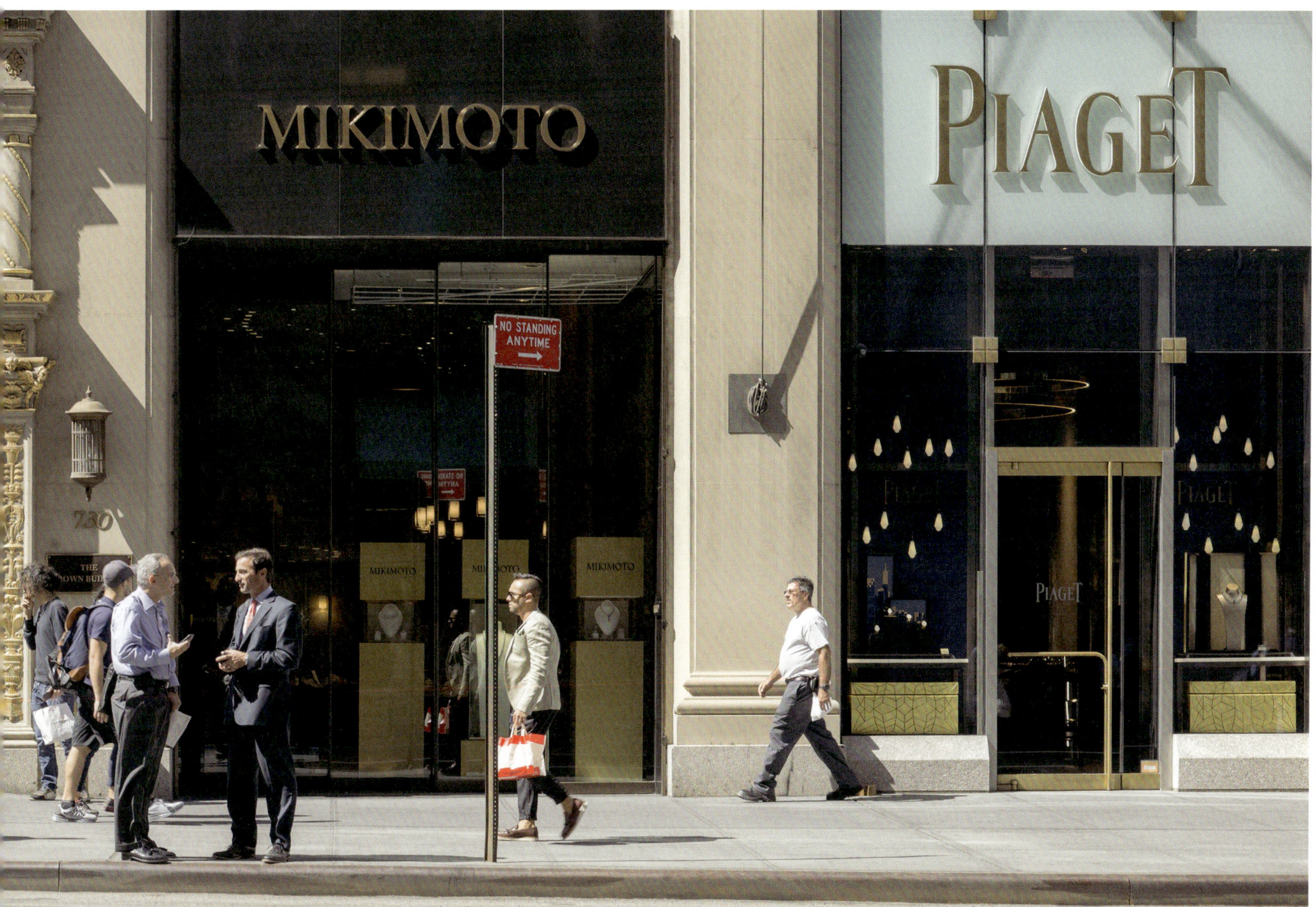
MIKIMOTO
PIAGET
NO STANDING
ANYTIME
730
THE
MIKIMOTO
MIKIMOTO
MIKIMOTO
PIAGET
PIAGET
PIAGET

68   5th Avenue 42, 2018

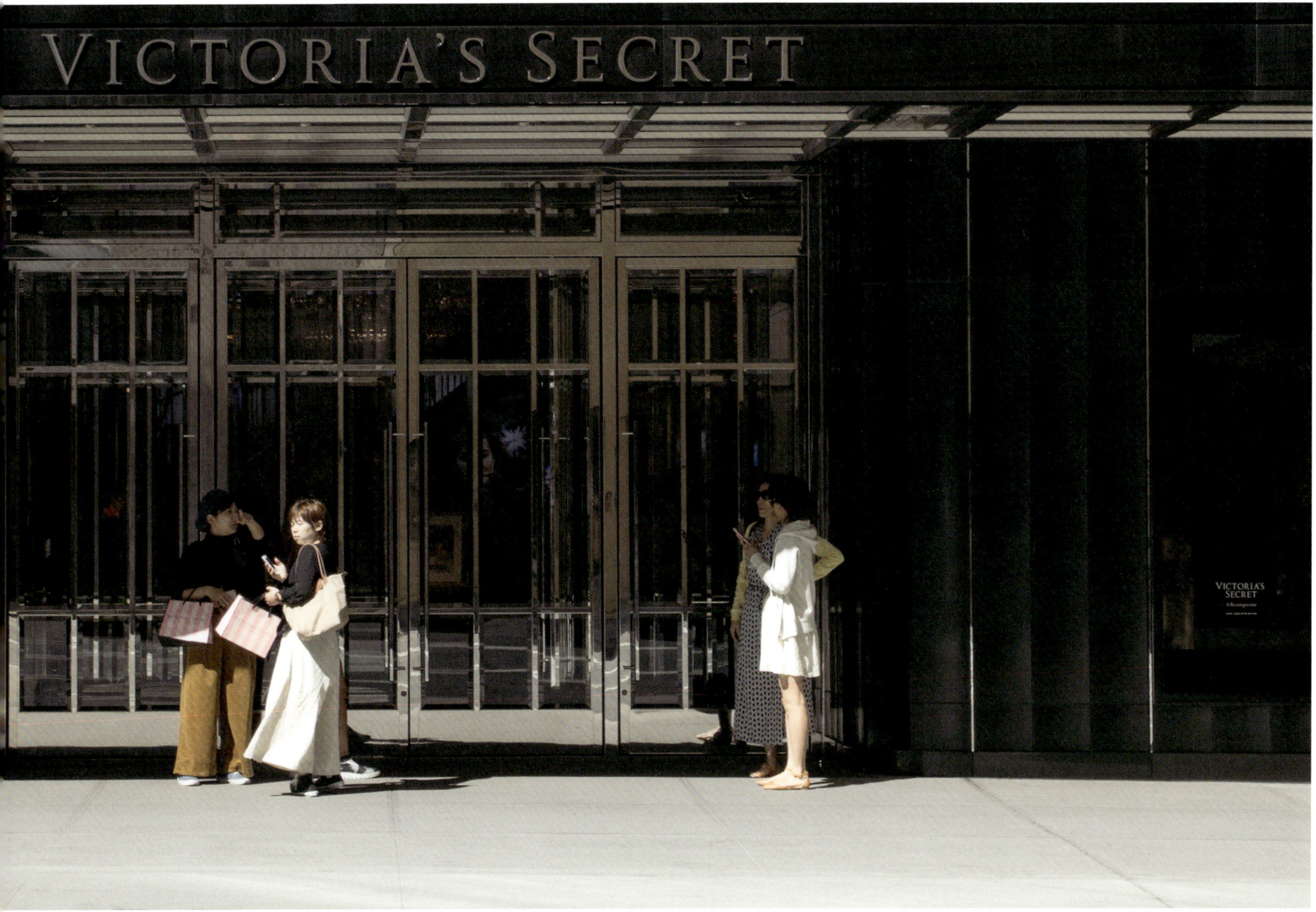

VICTORIA'S SECRET
VICTORIA'S SECRET

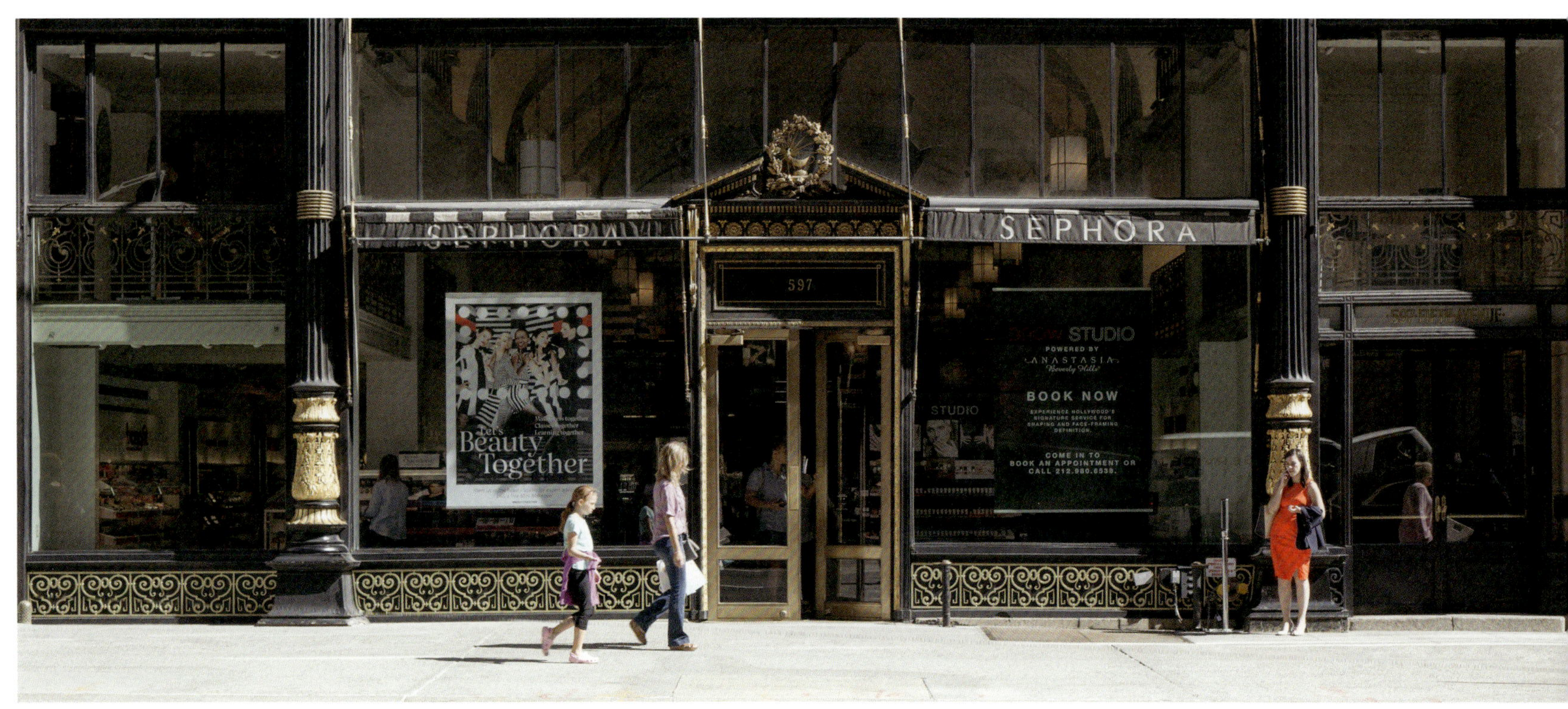

SEPHORA
SEPHORA
597
STUDIO
POWERED BY
ANASTASIA
Beverly Hills
BOOK NOW
COME IN TO
BOOK AN APPOINTMENT OR
CALL 212.980.6538.
STUDIO
Let's
Beauty
Together

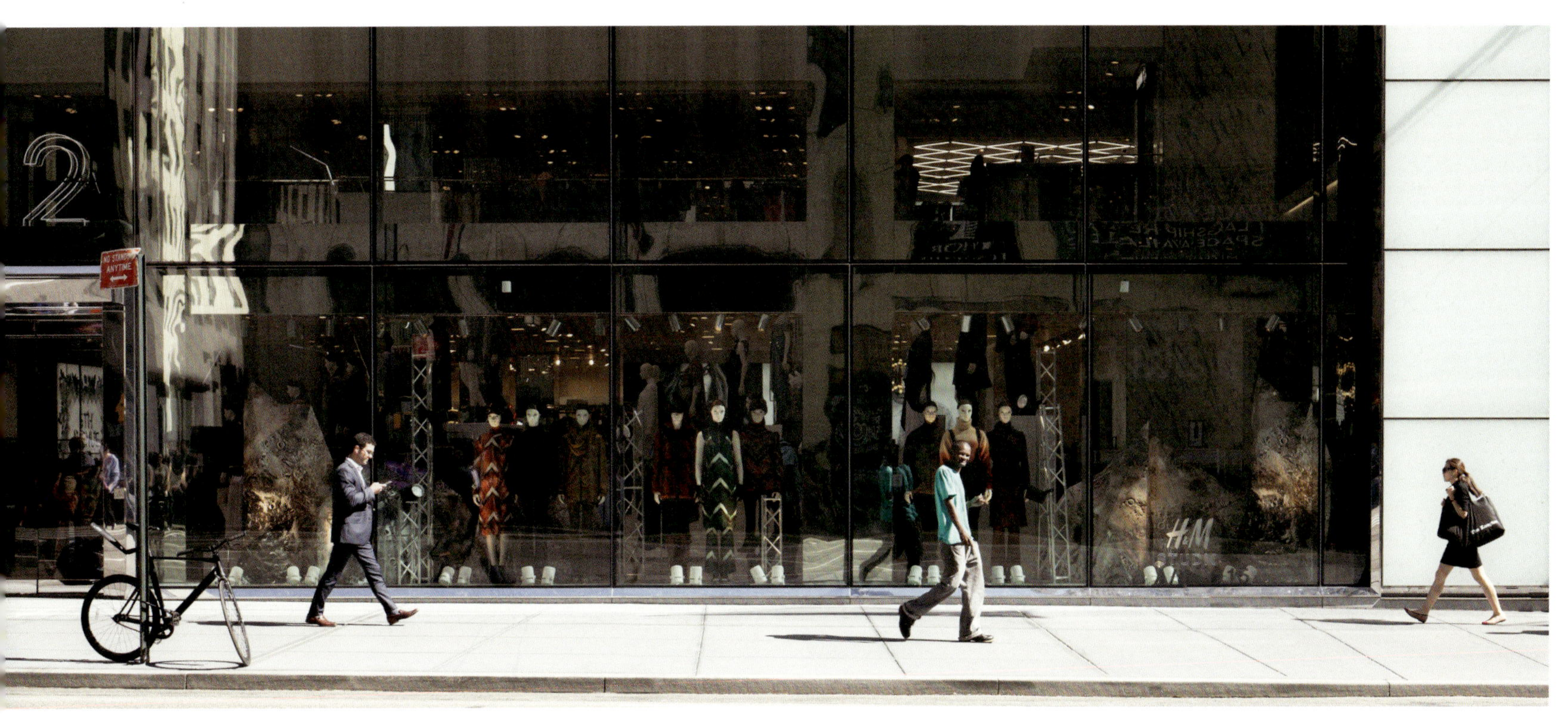

5th Avenue 28, 2016　　71

New York ist für mich eine faszinierende Stadt, in der Menschen aus vielen Nationen und Kulturen zusammentreffen. Diese multikulturelle Gesellschaft inspiriert meine künstlerische Arbeit bereits seit vielen Jahren. Eine besondere Bedeutung haben dabei die Subway-Stationen. Die New York Subway wurde 1904 eröffnet und zählt damit zu den ältesten U-Bahn-Netzen der Welt. Die heutige Anlage um die Pennsylvania Station stellt für mich mit ihrem Gewirr an unterirdischen Gängen einen besonderen Ort dar. Hier finde ich Motive für meine Fotografien und Videoinstallationen. Menschen mit diversen kulturellen Hintergründen treffen hier wie auf einer Bühne aufeinander. Ihre Bewegungen und unterschiedlichen Geschwindigkeiten sind spürbar, und es werden Einzelschicksale oder Geschichten des zwischenmenschlichen Lebens sichtbar.

For me, New York is a fascinating city where people from many nations and cultures meet. This multicultural society has inspired my artistic work for many years. The subway stations have a special meaning. The New York Subway was opened in 1904 and is one of the oldest subway networks in the world. Today's complex around Pennsylvania Station, with its maze of underground corridors, is a special place for me. Here I find motifs for my photographs and video installations. Here, people from vastly diverse backgrounds meet as if on a stage. Their different movements and speeds are perceptible, and individual fates or stories of interpersonal lives become visible.

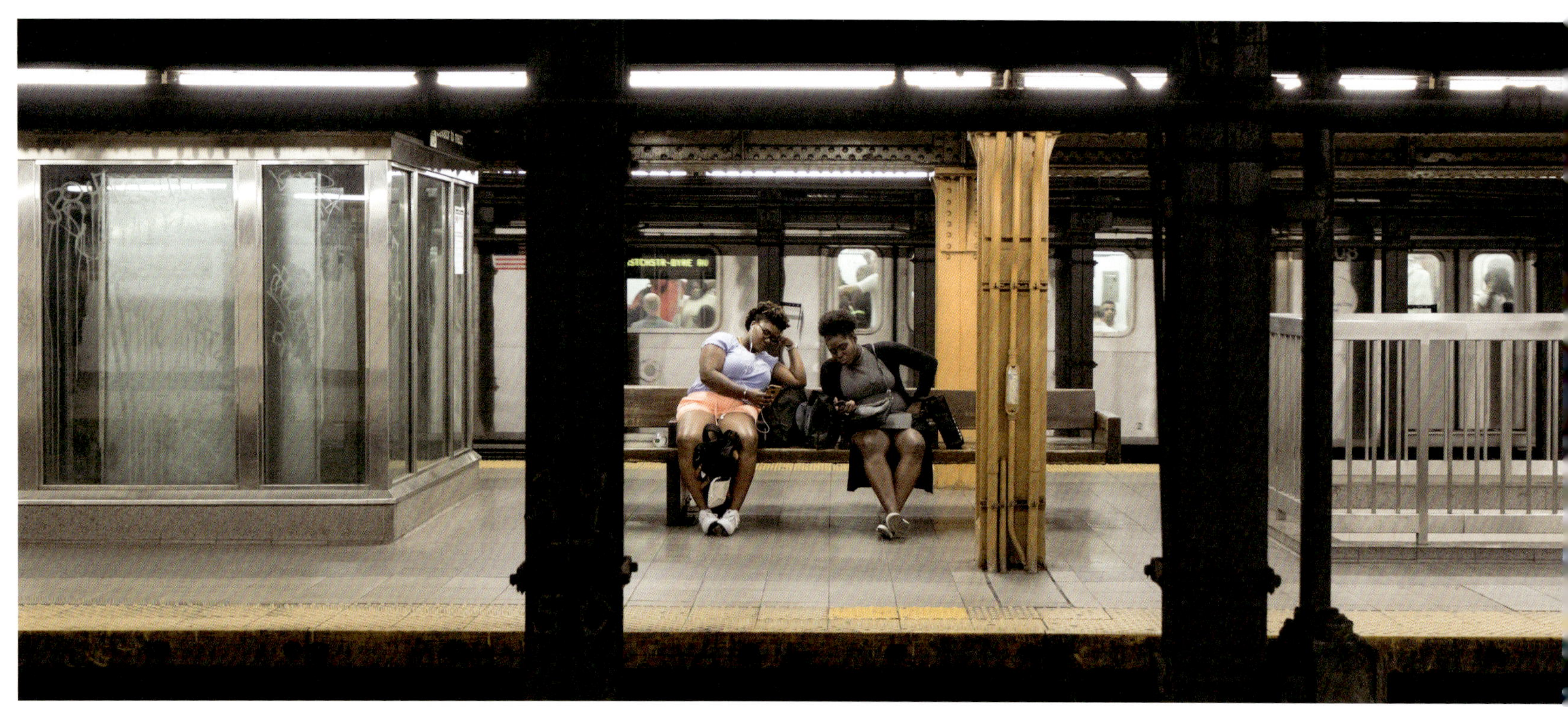

74   Subway 1, 2018

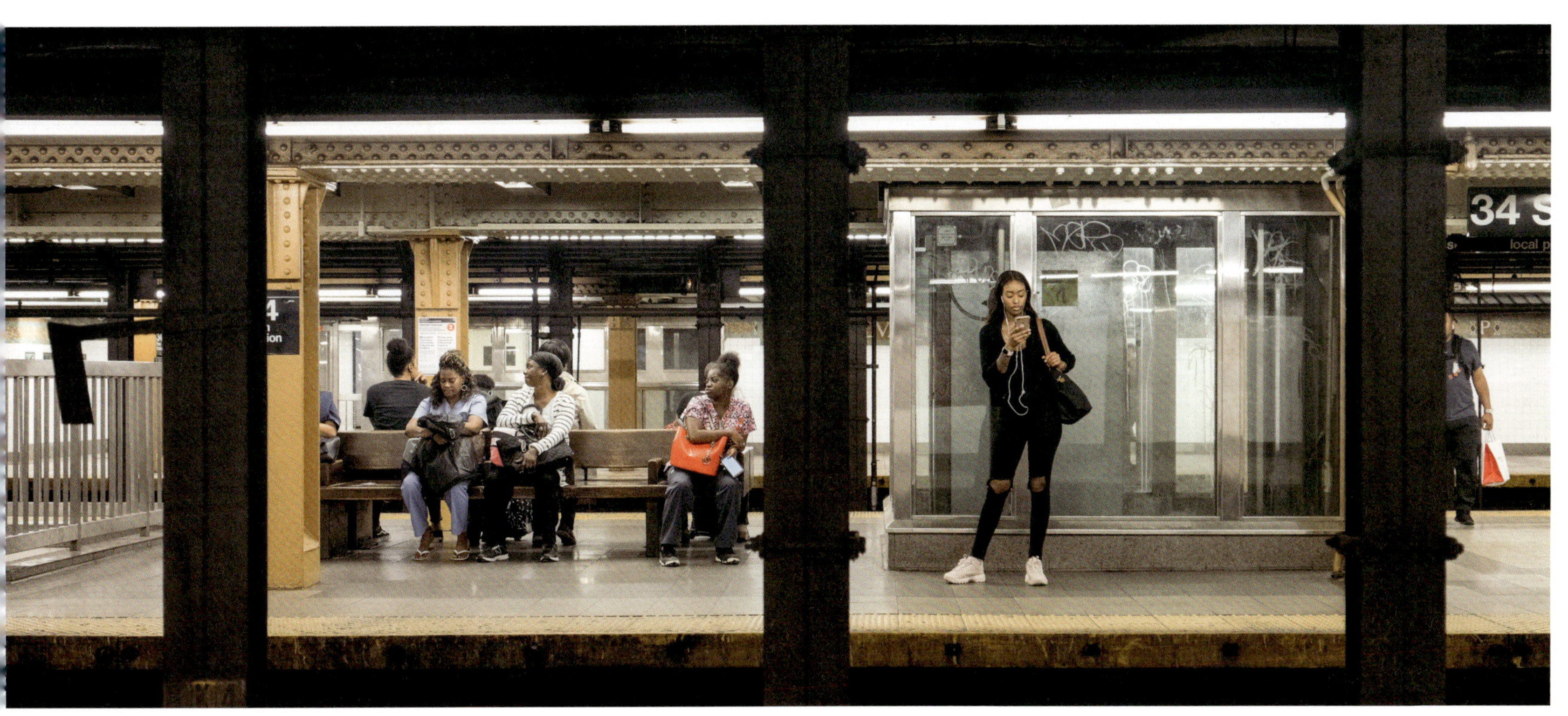

Subway 36, 2018

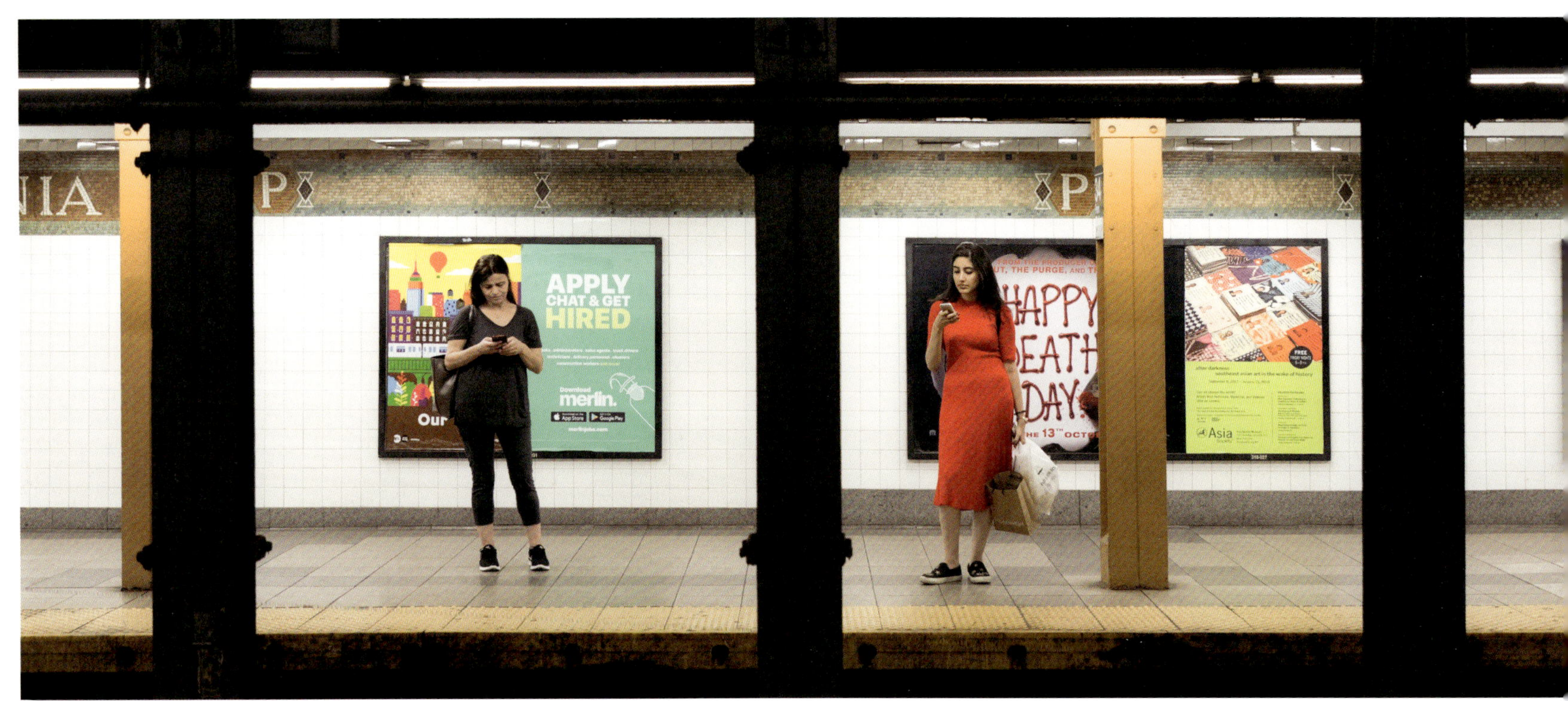

76   Subway 5, 2018

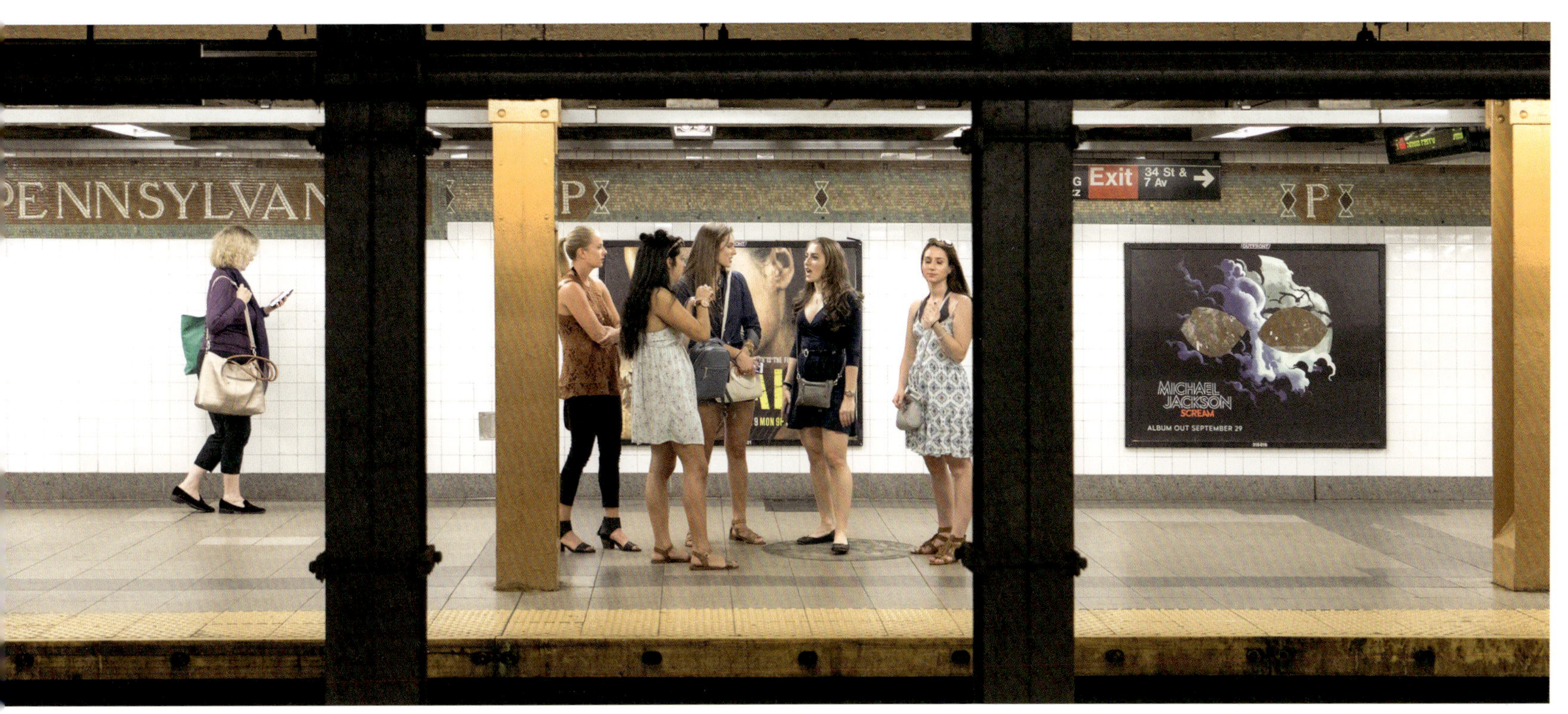
PENNSYLVAN
P
P
Exit
34 St &
7 Av
MICHAEL
JACKSON
SCREAM
ALBUM OUT SEPTEMBER 29

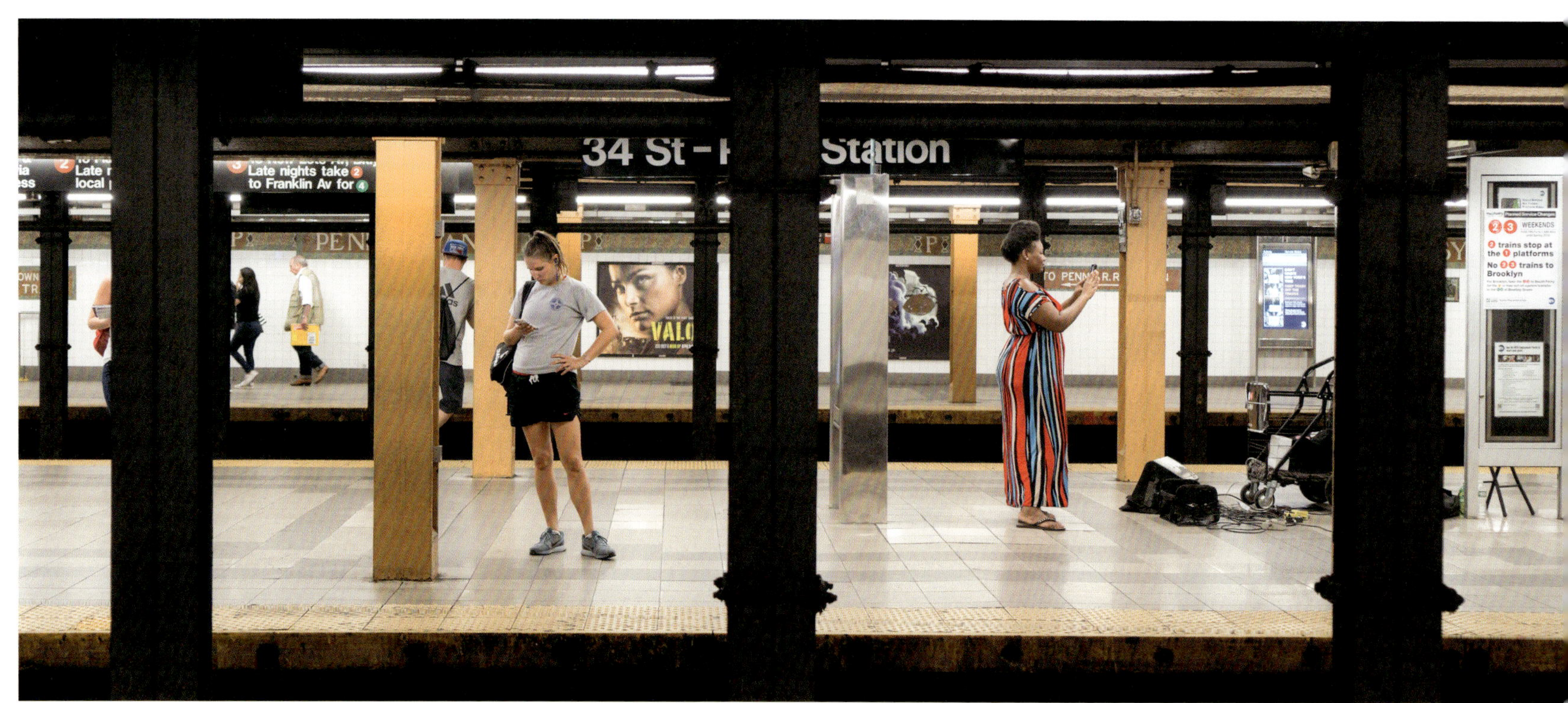

34 St - Penn Station
2 Late nights take
to Franklin Av for 4
3 To New York Fri Evening
Late nights take 2
to Franklin Av for 4
2 3 WEEKENDS
2 trains stop at
the 1 platforms
No 2 3 trains to
Brooklyn
TO PENN R.R.
VALO

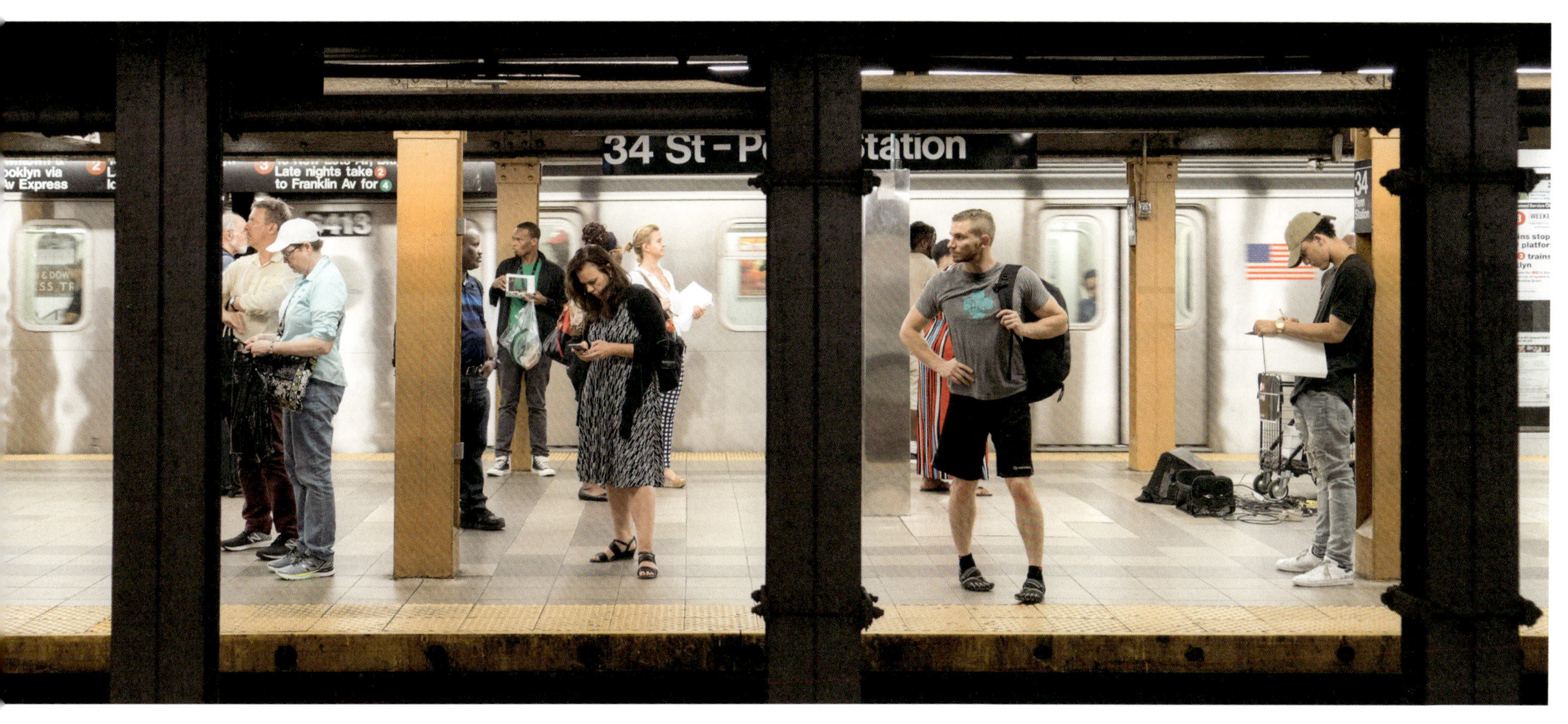

Subway 3, 2018   79

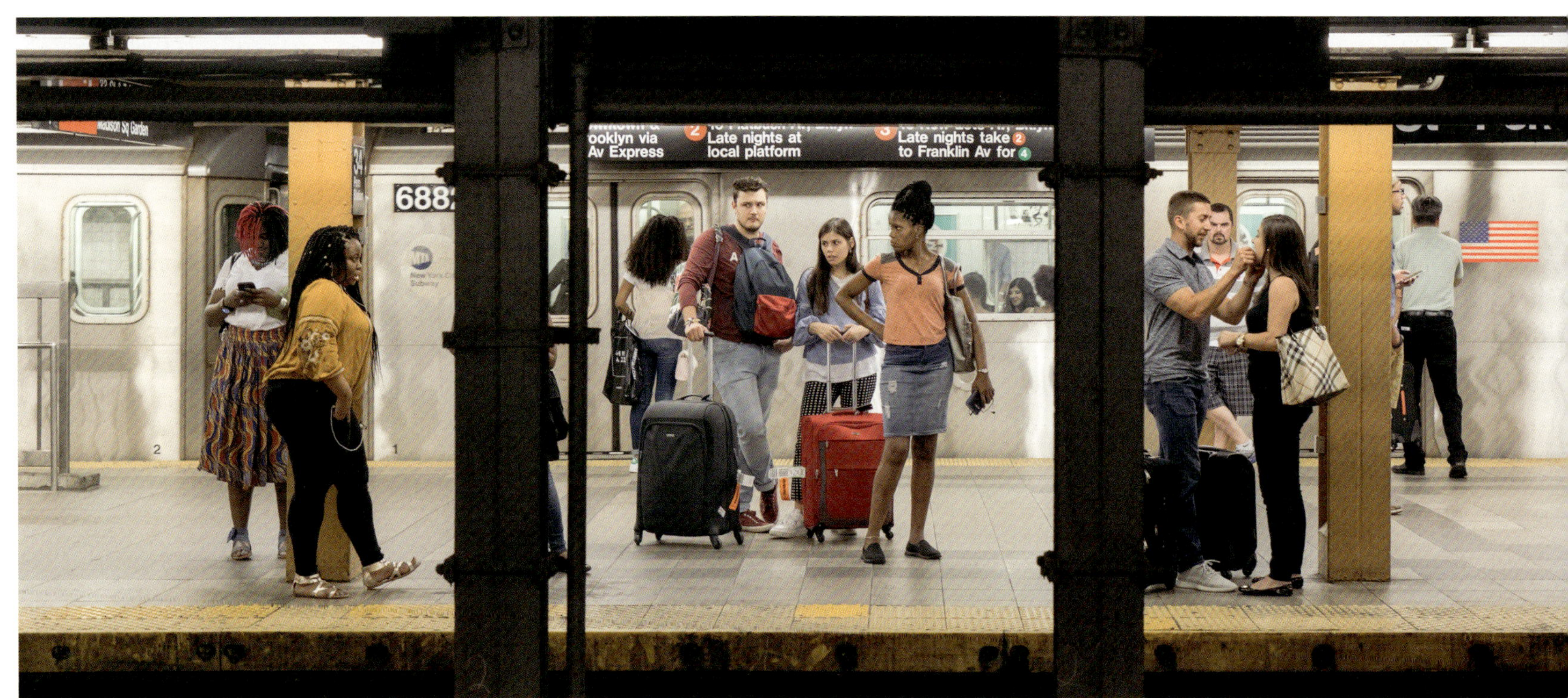

     Subway 9, 2018

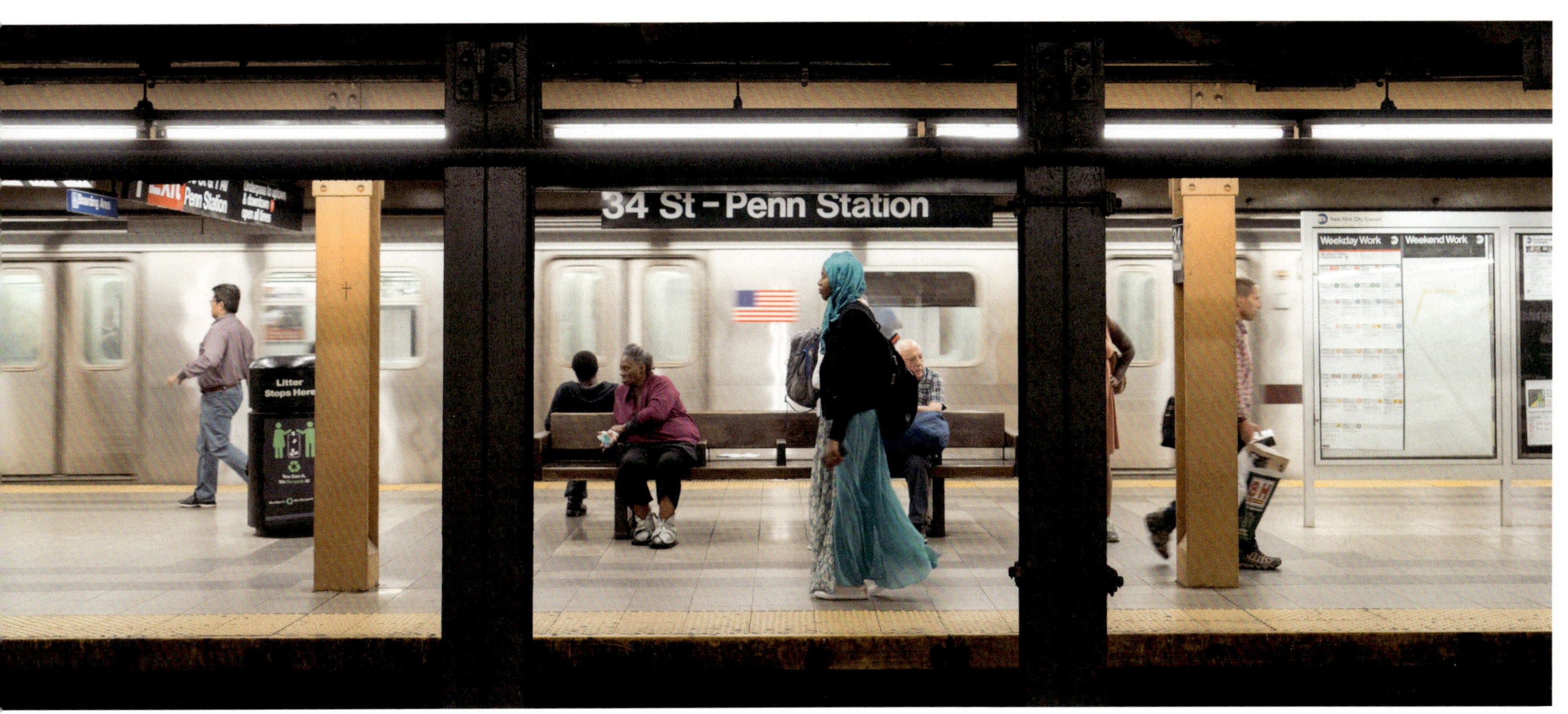
Boarding Area
EXIT
Penn Station
34 St - Penn Station
Litter
Stops Here
Weekday Work
Weekend Work
New York City Transit

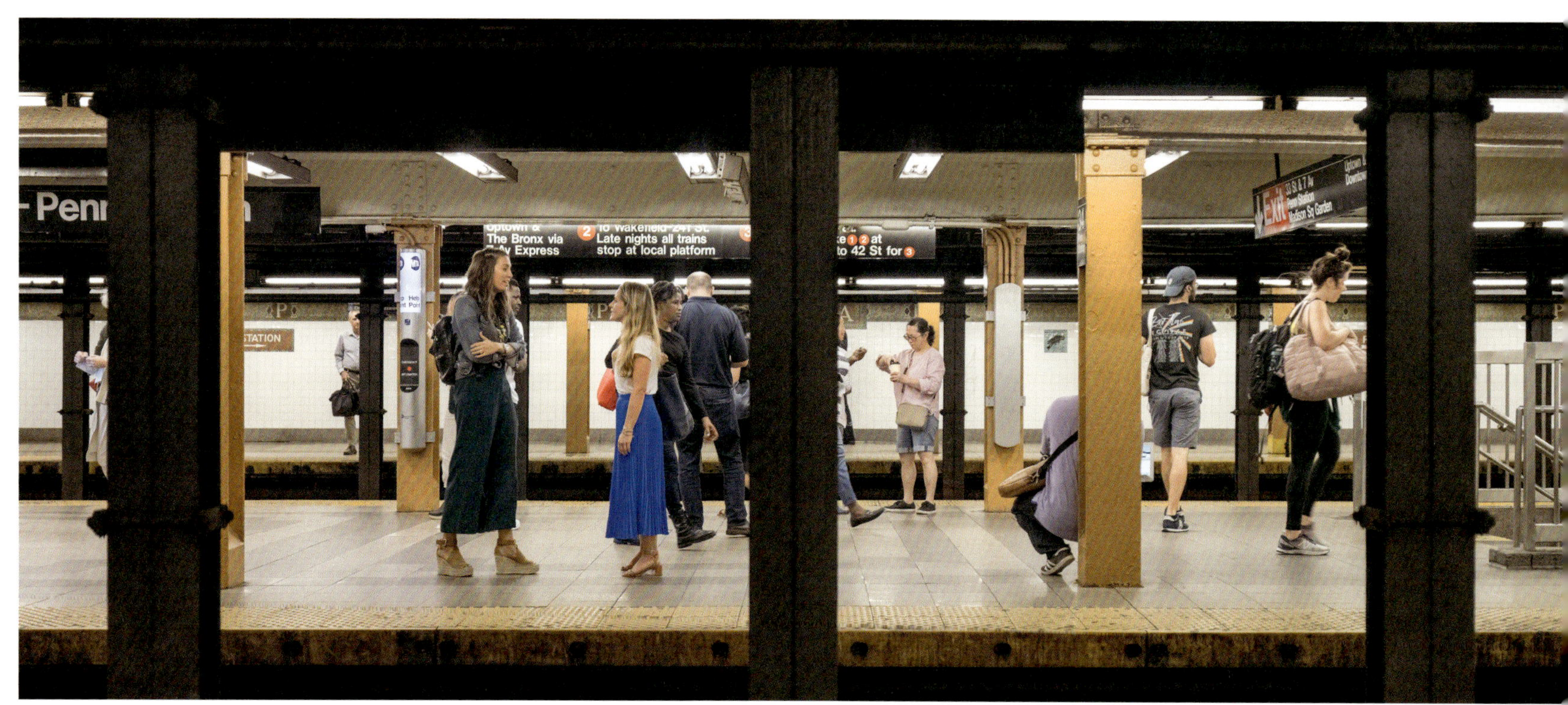
Penn
Uptown &
The Bronx via
7 Av Express
2 To Wakefield–241 St
Late nights all trains
stop at local platform
1 2 at
to 42 St for 3
1 2 3 A & 7 Av
Exit
Madison Sq Garden
Uptown &
Downtown
STATION

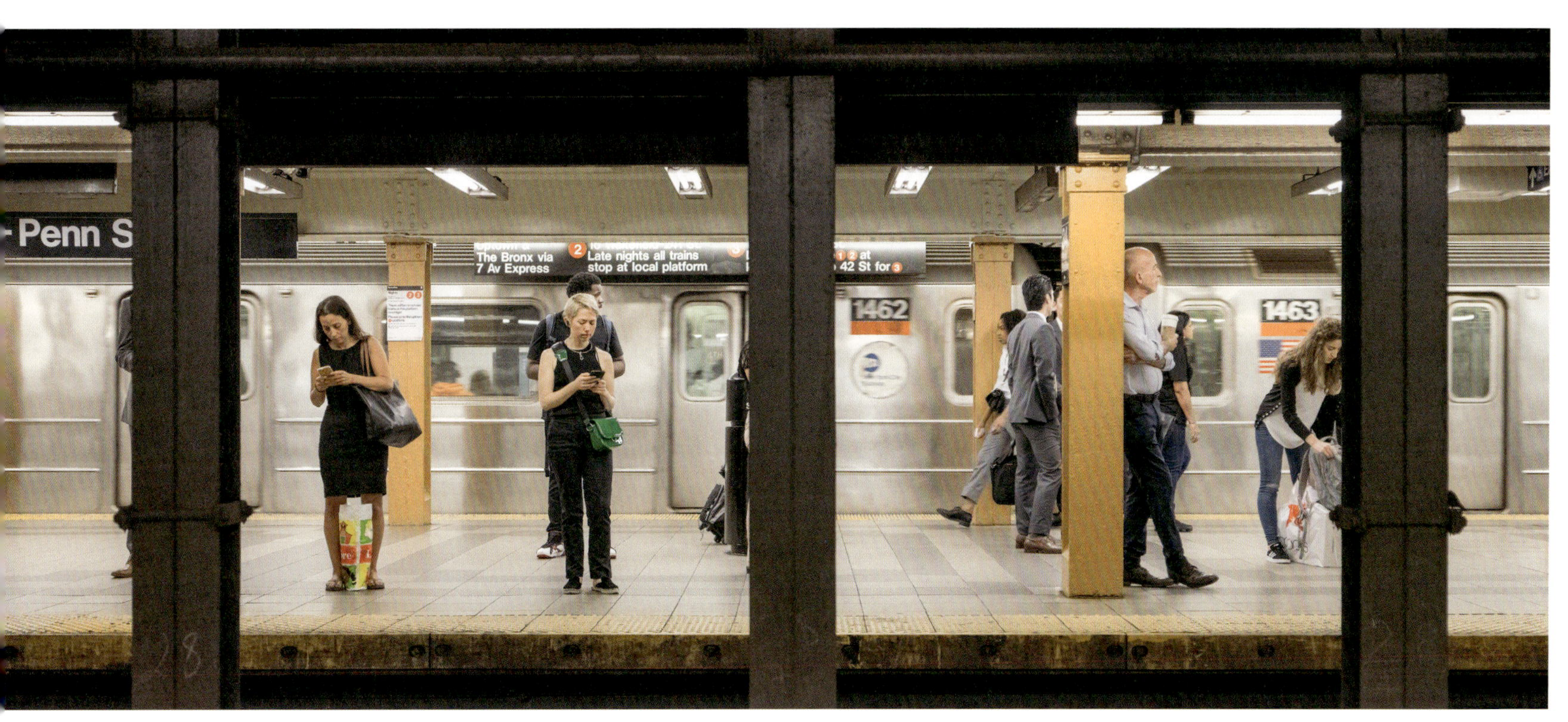
Penn S
The Bronx via
7 Av Express
2
Late nights all trains
stop at local platform
42 St for 3
1462
1463

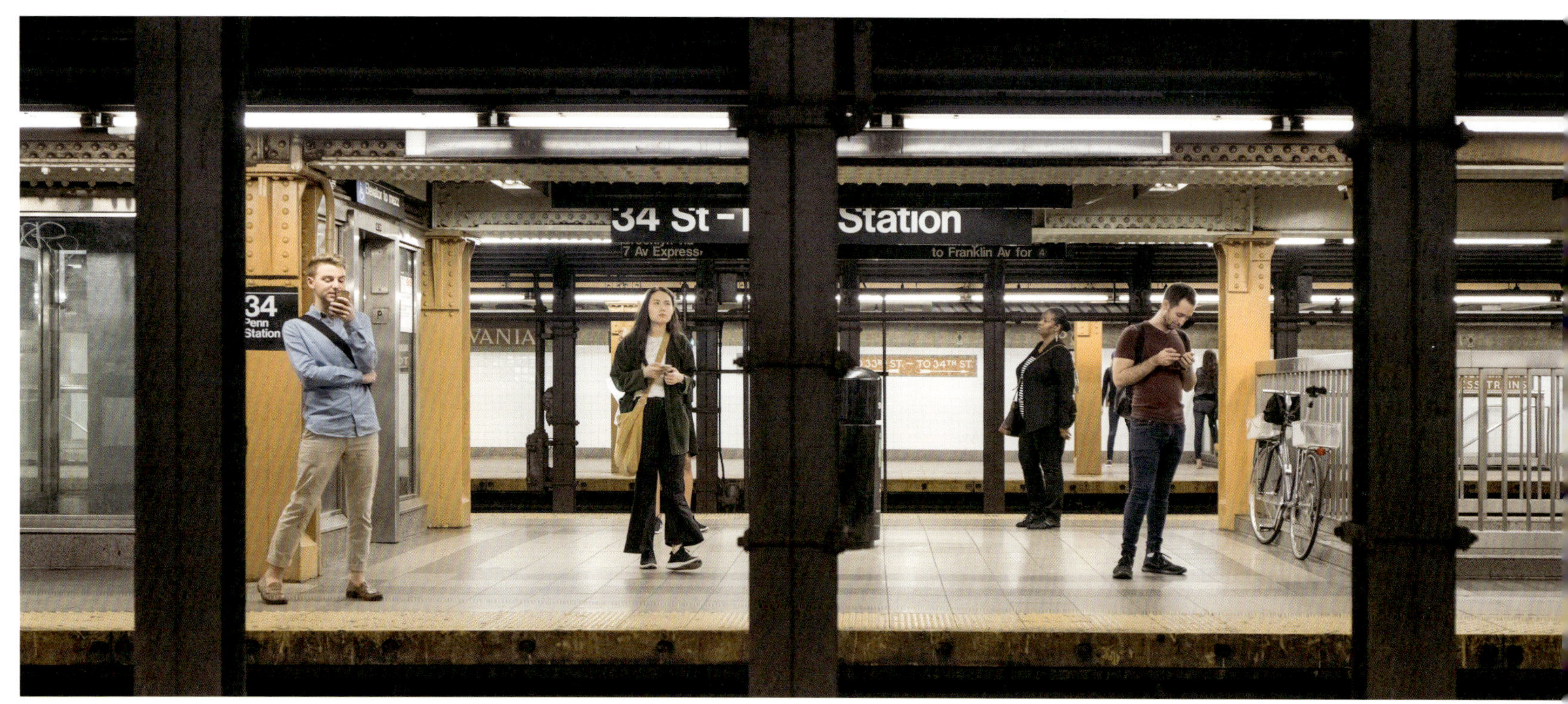

84   Subway 88, 2018

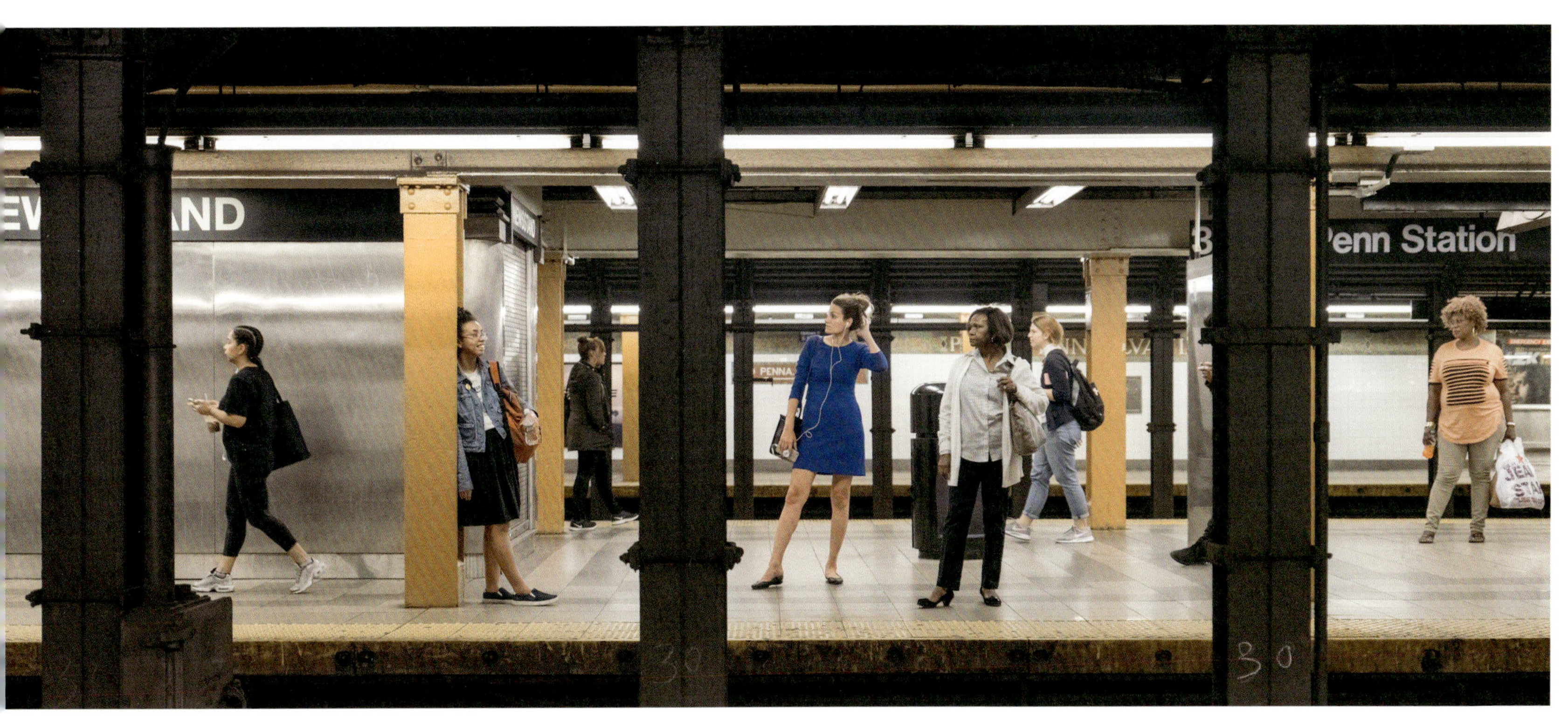
Penn Station

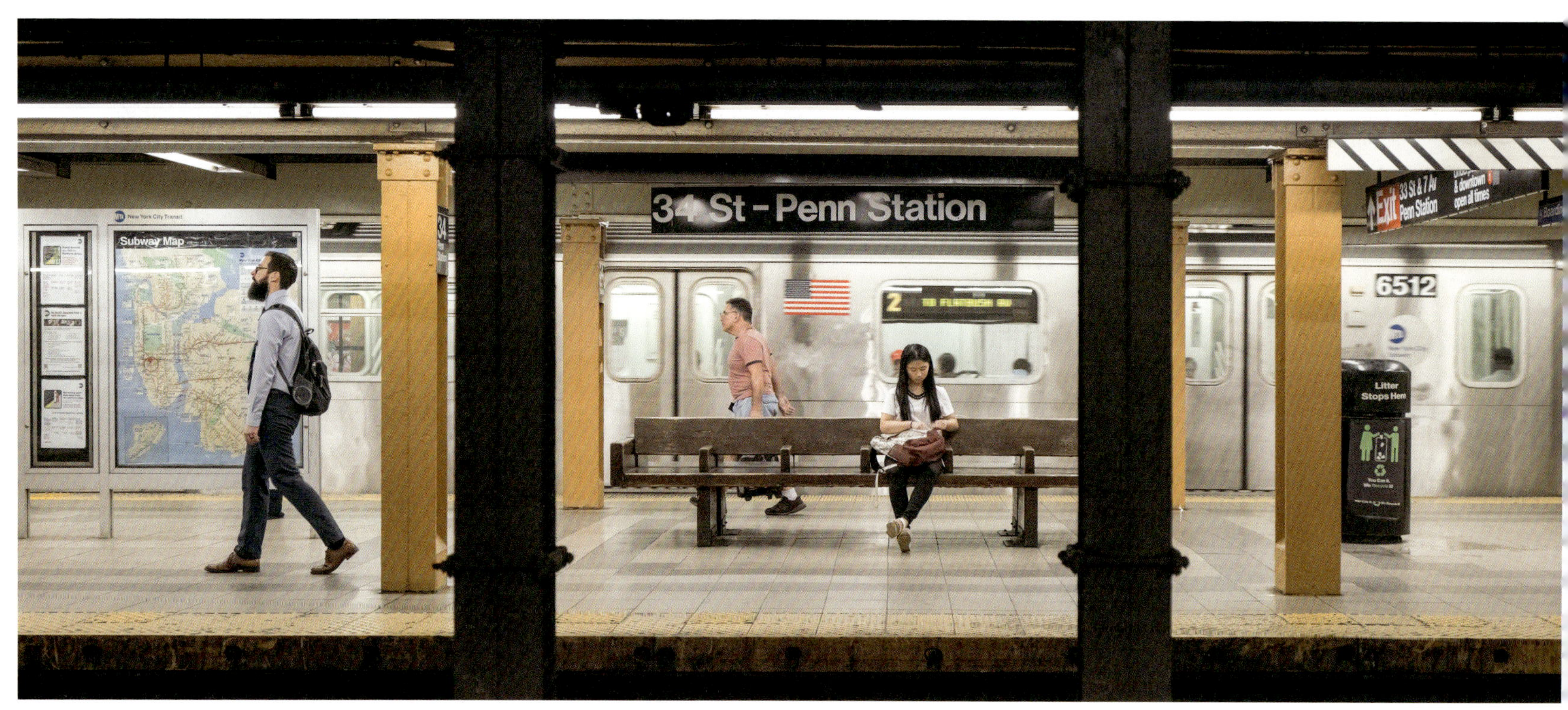

86   Subway 102, 2018

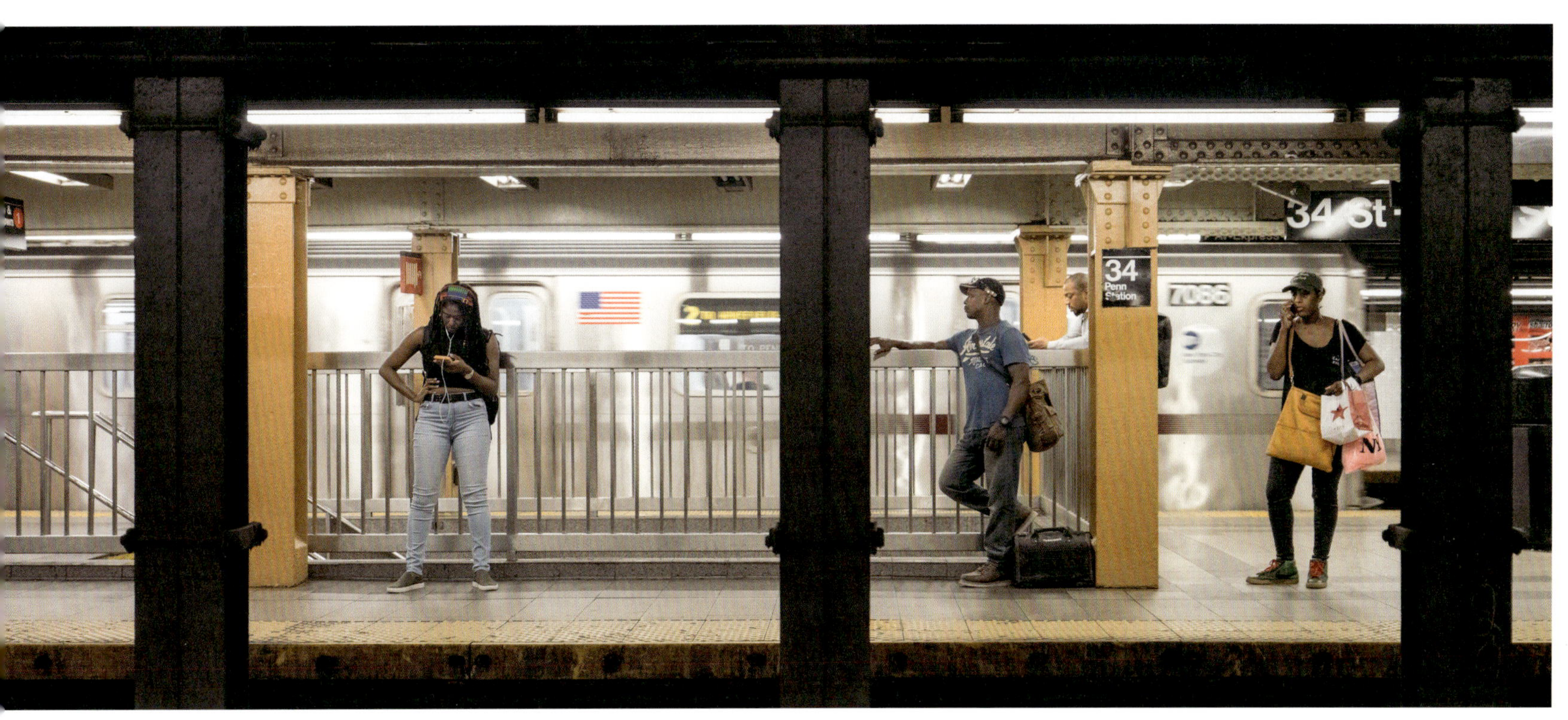

34 St
Penn Station
34
7066

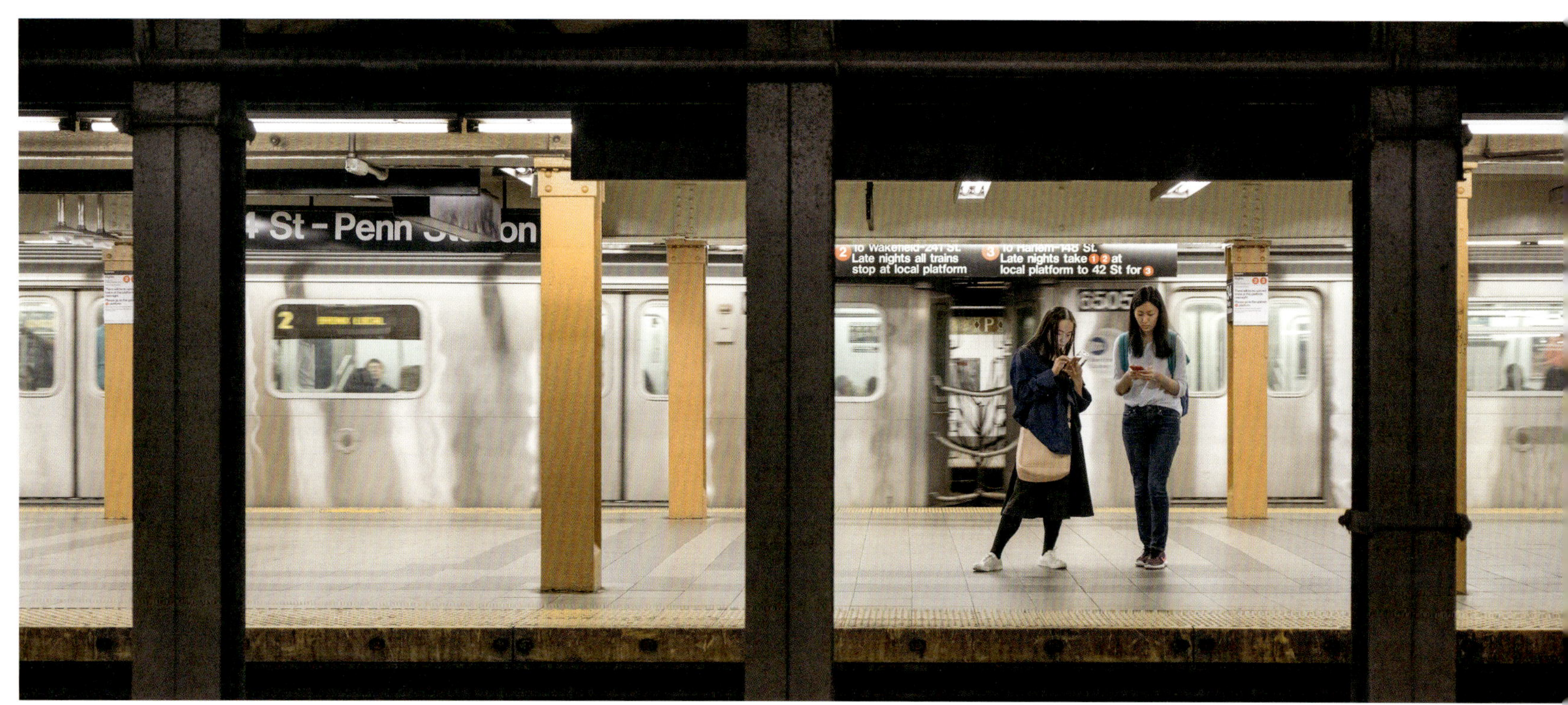
St - Penn Station
To Wakefield-241 St
Late nights all trains
stop at local platform
To Harlem-148 St.
Late nights take 1 2 at
local platform to 42 St for 3
2

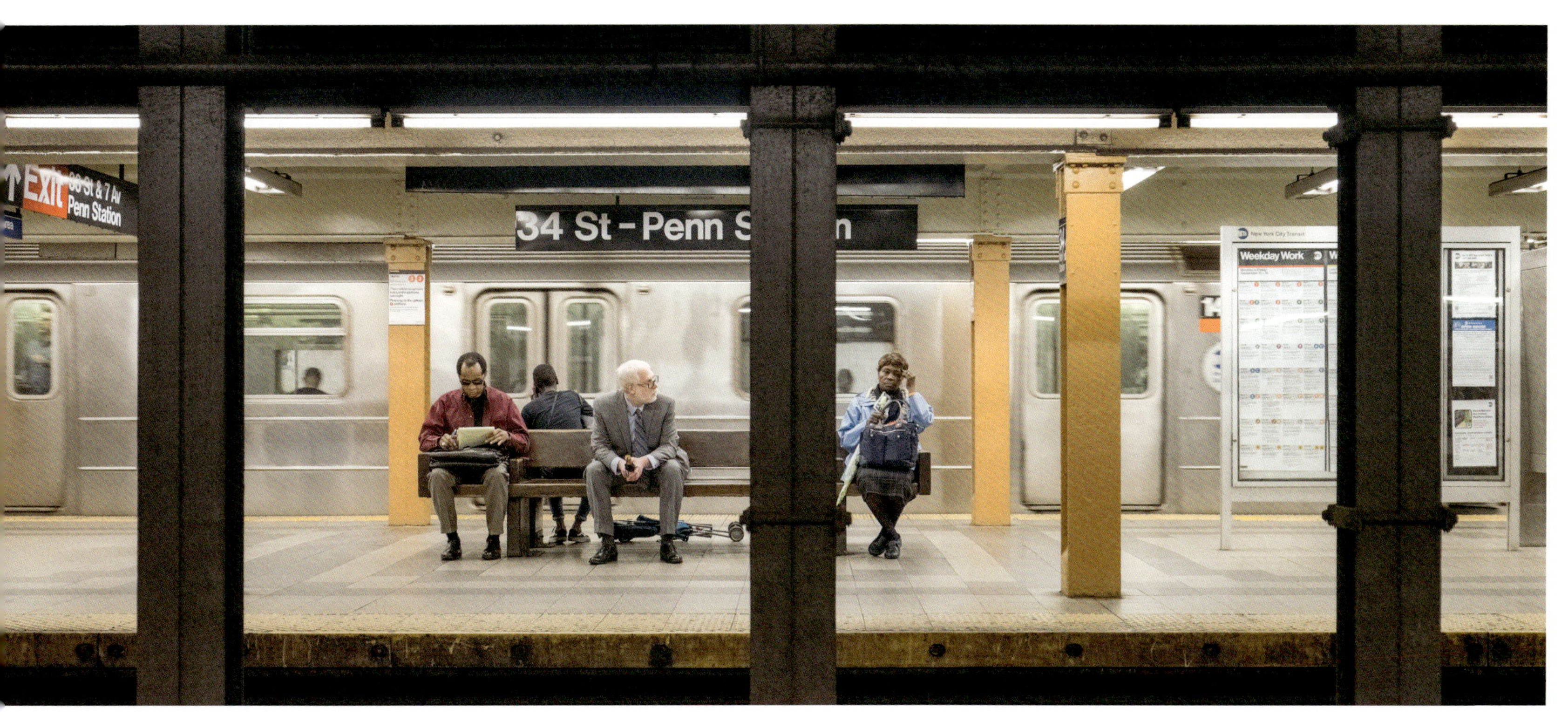

Exit
34 St & 7 Av
Penn Station
34 St - Penn Station
New York City Transit
Weekday Work

General Motors, 2012
2-channel video installation, HD
4:00 min.

Zwei Kameras beobachten den Eingang zum Apple Store vor dem General Motors Gebäude in New York. Die Menschen im rechten Bild streben zu dem gläsernen Eingang und fahren mit einem Aufzug in den unterirdisch gelegenen Apple Store. Konsumorientiert folgen sie instinktiv ihrem Wunsch, stets das neueste Smartphone, die beste Apple Watch oder das größte Tablet zu besitzen, um mit diesen Geräten ständig online und erreichbar zu sein. Mittels GPS finden sie zumindest physisch ihre Position überall auf der Welt, machen sich damit aber auch jederzeit lokalisierbar. Die Videoinstallation erinnert an den Roman *1984*, in dem George Orwell die Dystopie eines totalitären Überwachungs- und Präventionsstaates beschreibt, aber auch an den Film *Die Zeitmaschine* des Regisseurs George Pal aus dem Jahr 1960, der auf dem gleichnamigen Roman von H. G. Wells aus dem Jahre 1895 basiert. In diesem Film ertönt ein Alarm, ähnlich den Polizeisirenen in Manhattan, woraufhin die Menschen wie hypnotisiert in das sakrale Gebäude der Morlocks laufen und dort von diesen verspeist werden.

Two cameras observe the entrance to the Apple Store in front of the General Motors building on Manhattan's Fifth Avenue. The people in the picture on the right are striving to get to the glass entrance and take an elevator to the underground Apple Store. Consumption-oriented, they instinctively follow their desire to own the latest smartphone, the best Apple Watch or the biggest tablet, in order to be constantly online and reachable with these devices. By using GPS, they can at least physically find their position anywhere in the world — but they can also be located at any time. The video installation recalls the novel *1984*, in which George Orwell describes the dystopia of a totalitarian surveillance and prevention state, as well as the 1960 film *The Time Machine*, by director George Pal, based on the novel of the same title by H. G. Wells from 1895. In this film an alarm sounds, similar to the noise of police sirens in Manhattan, whereupon people are hypnotized, enter the sacred building of the Morlocks, and are eaten there by them.

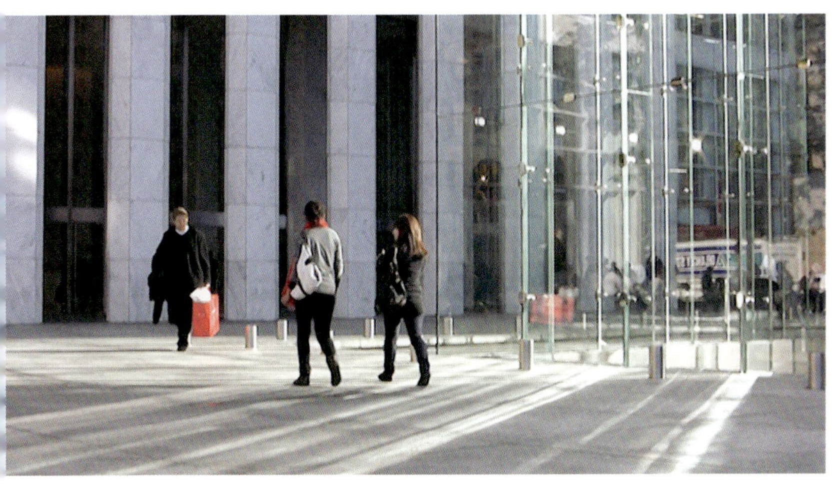 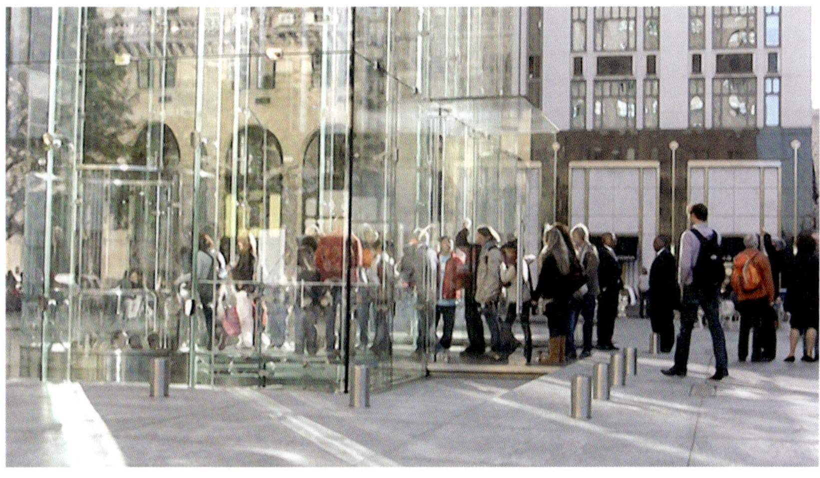

Subway, 2015
2-channel video installation, HD
2:46 min.

Die New York Subway wurde am 27. Oktober 1904 eröffnet und zählt damit zu den ältesten U-Bahn-Netzen der Welt. Die 2-Kanal-Videoinstallation zeigt Penn Station in zwei Bildern, die zusammen eine Panoramaansicht ergeben. Menschen aller Nationen treffen in diesem medial erschaffenen Bühnenraum zusammen. Sie bewegen sich in unterschiedlichen Geschwindigkeiten. Die lang andauernde und statische Beobachtung der Menschen führt zu einer Auseinandersetzung mit der eigenen und der fremden Zeit.

The subway network in New York was opened on 27 October 1904, making it one of the oldest in the world. The 2-channel video installation shows Penn Station in two images, which provide a panoramic view. People of all nations meet in this media-created stage space. They move at different speeds. The long-lasting and static observation of the people leads to a confrontation with one's own time and that of others.

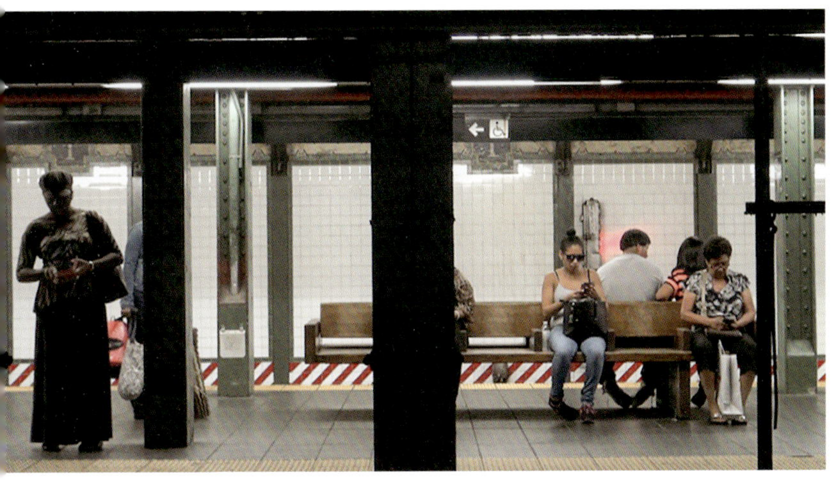 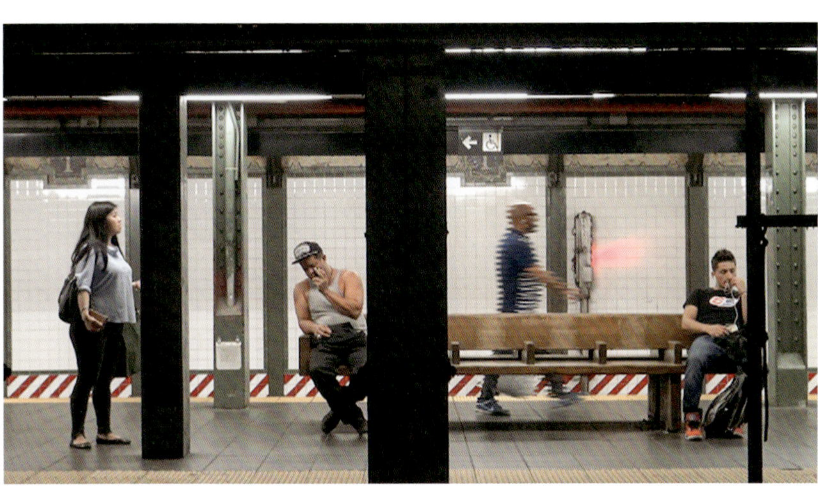

Manhattan Bridge, 2014
2-channel video installation, HD
8:30 min.

Die 2-Kanal-Videoinstallation *Manhattan Bridge* zeigt eine Fahrt über die Brooklyn Bridge von Brooklyn nach Soho mit Blick auf die Manhattan Bridge. Die Manhattan Bridge überquert den East River und verbindet die beiden Stadtteile Brooklyn und Lower Manhattan. Der in der Videoinstallation medial erschaffene Bühnenraum lebt von dem Spiel der Geschwindigkeiten. Die Performance der statischen Architekturelemente ergibt sich auf natürliche Weise durch das Tempo der Kamerafahrt. Die visuelle Erfahrung von Raum und Zeit führt durch die asynchrone Projektion und durch die stimmungsvolle Akustik zu einer neuen medialen Raumwahrnehmung.

The 2-channel video installation *Manhattan Bridge* shows a tour across the Brooklyn Bridge from Brooklyn to Soho with a view of the Manhattan Bridge. The Manhattan Bridge crosses the East River and connects the two districts, Brooklyn and Lower Manhattan. The stage space created in the video installation is driven by the interaction of speeds. The performance of the static architectural elements results naturally from the speed of the camera movement. The visual experience of space and time leads through the asynchronous projection and the atmospheric acoustics to a new media perception of space.

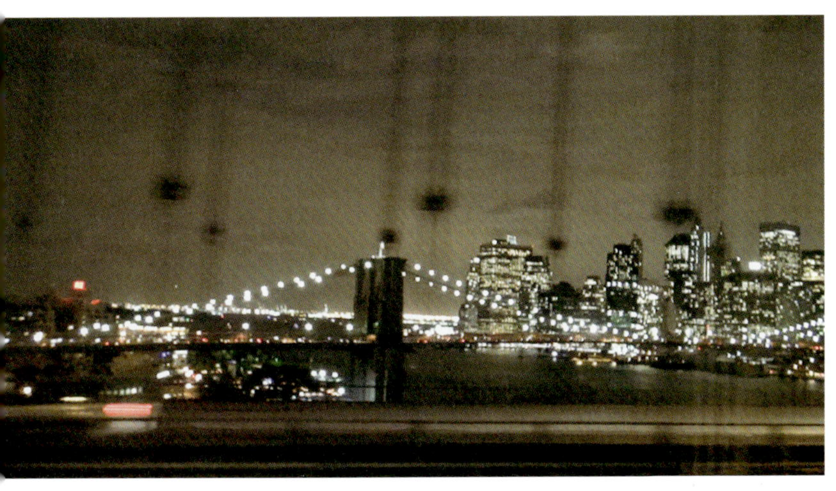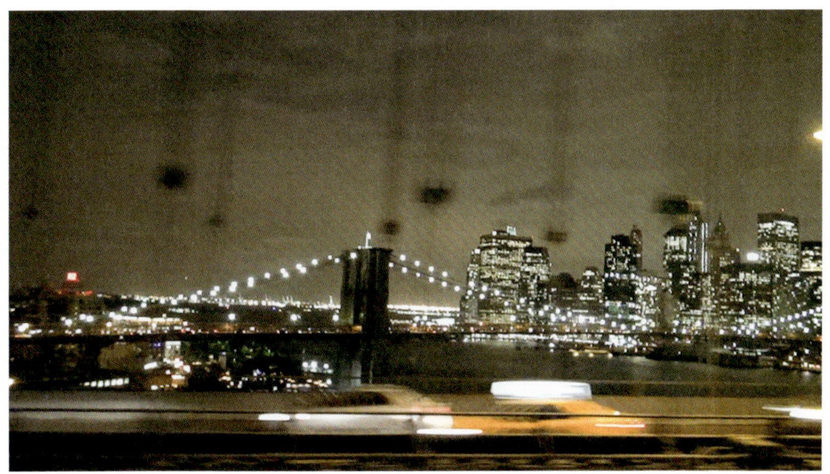

Manhattan, 2014
2-channel video installation, HD
Sound: Gudrun Kemsa, Peter Thoma
8:50 min.

Die 2-Kanal-Videoinstallation *Manhattan* zeigt eine von einem offenen Doppeldeckerbus aufgenommene Kamerafahrt durch Manhattan. Sie führt entlang des Broadways, um den Times Square herum und anschließend durch die 42nd Street. Durch die erhöhte Blickposition werden die Straßenschluchten erlebbar. Der Blick des Betrachters fällt tief in die Straßen und Gebäude hinein. Durch die Bewegung fließt die Architektur scheinbar ineinander. Der visuelle Raum öffnet sich durch die Wechselwirkung der Geschwindigkeit. Die Bildperformance der statischen Architekturelemente ergibt sich auf natürliche Weise durch das Tempo der Kamerafahrt. Die akustische Begleitung unterstützt und fördert die Raumerfahrung. Durch diese Videoinstallation entsteht eine neue visuelle Wahrnehmung von Raum und Zeit.

The 2-channel video installation Manhattan shows a camera ride through Manhattan recorded from an open double-decker bus: along Broadway, around Times Square, and then down 42nd Street. From the elevated viewing position, the canyons of the streets can be experienced. The viewer's gaze falls deep into the streets and buildings. Through the movement, the architectural structures seem to flow into each other. The visual space opens up through the interaction with speed. The image performance of the static architectural elements results naturally from the speed of the camera movement. The acoustic accompaniment supports and promotes the spatial experience. This video installation creates a new visual perception of space and time.

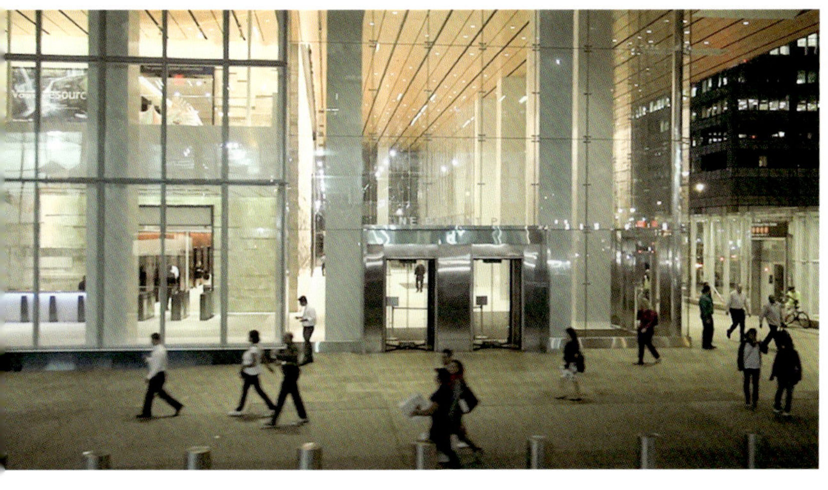 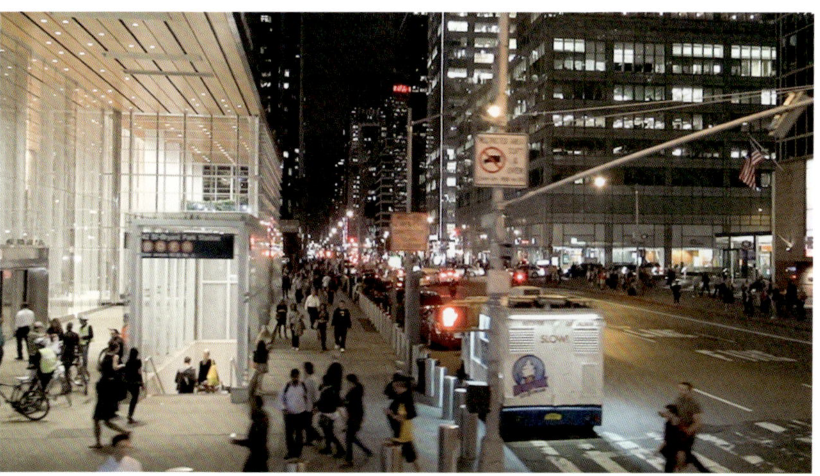

**Danke an /
Thanks to**

meine Familie / my family:
Brigitte Obetz, Richard Obetz, New York City
Sigrid Kemsa, Viola Kemsa, Jürgen Möller-Kemsa

Bernd A. Lausberg, Düsseldorf
Volker Schräger-Enkirch, SIGMA, Düsseldorf
Gerd Stenmans, Mechthild Urmelt, HSL, Düsseldorf
Dr. Tayfun Belgin, Hagen
Dr. Marion Bornscheuer, Passau
Prof. Dr. Kai Uwe Schierz, Erfurt

     Manhattan Cruise, 2019, 2-channel video installation, HD, sound: Gudrun Kemsa, Paul Müller-Reyes, 8:30 min.

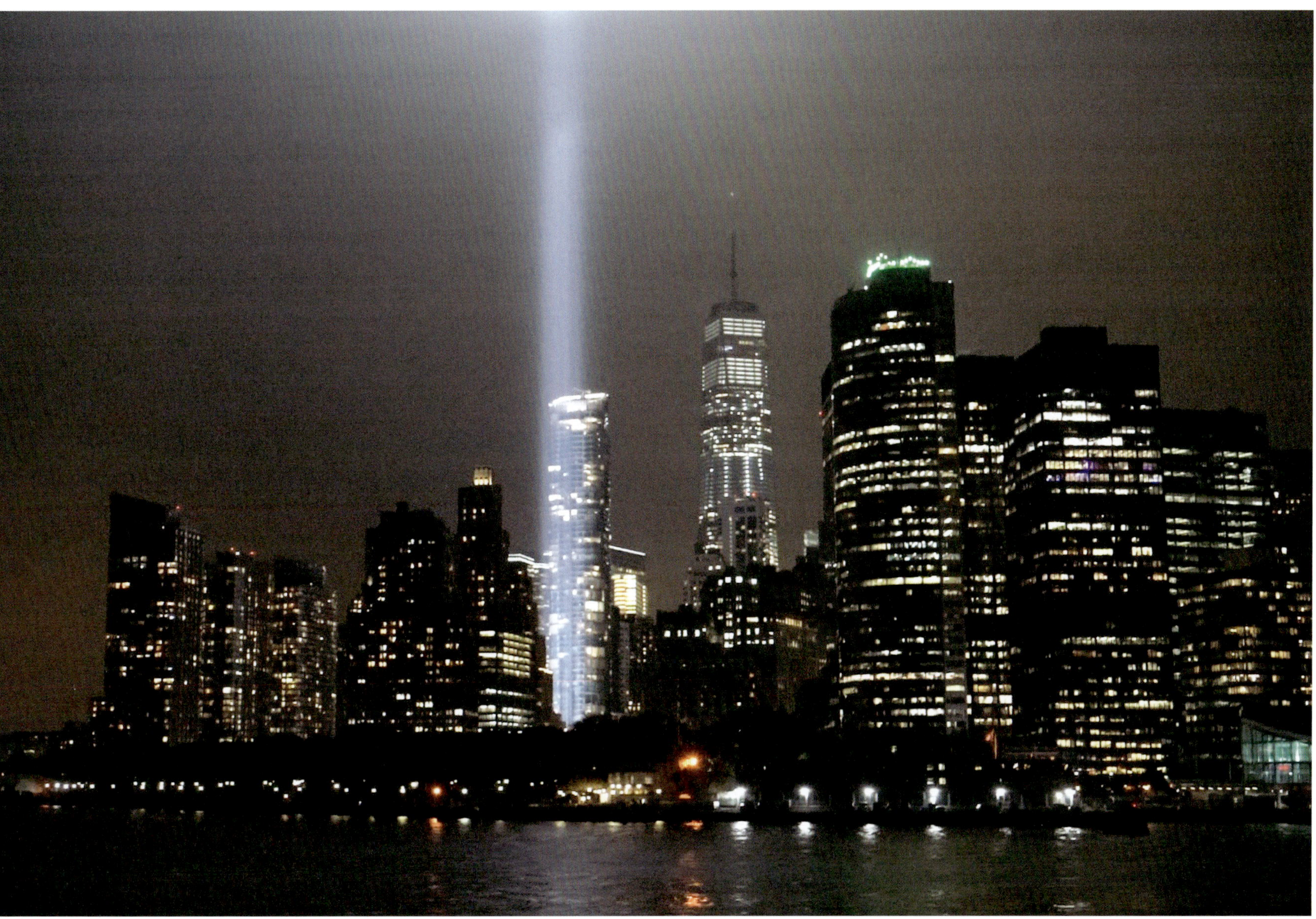

Gudrun Kemsa
1961 born in Datteln **1980–1990** Academy of Fine Arts Düsseldorf **1989** Travel Grant, Kunstverein für die Rheinlande und Westfalen, Düsseldorf **1995** New York Grant, Ernst-Poensgen-Foundation **1996–1997** Villa Massimo Grant, Rome **1999** Project Grant, ZKM, Karlsruhe **2000** 9th Marler Video Art Prize: Special Grant, Skulpturenmuseum Marl / Academy of Media Arts, Cologne since **2001** Professorship for Moving Images and Photography, University of Applied Sciences, Krefeld. Lives in Düsseldorf.

Solo Exhibitions (Selection)
2019 *Move in Time*, Kunsthalle im Kunsthaus Nexus, Saalfelden | *Moving Portraits*, Salzburg Museum **2018** *Die Welt als Bühne*, Galerie Bernd A. Lausberg, Düsseldorf **2016** *Die Welt als Bühne* (Carole Feuerman, Veronika Veit), Haus Beda, Bitburg **2014** *Lausberg Contemporary*, Armory Art Center, Greenfield Gallery, West Palm Beach, Florida **2013** *Urban Stage*, Rheinisches Landesmuseum Bonn **2012** *Urban Stage*, Kunstmuseum Ahlen **2011** *Urban Stage*, Kunstverein Ingolstadt / Städtische Galerie Waldkraiburg **2010** *Urban Stage*, Landesgalerie Linz **2008** *Moving Images*, Neues Kunstforum, Cologne **2007** *Moving Images*, Städtische Galerie, Iserlohn / Galerie Rachel Haferkamp, Cologne / Kunstverein Ruhr e.V., Essen / Jenaer Kunstverein e.V., Jena **2006** *Moving Images*, Samuelis Baumgarte Galerie, Bielefeld | *Public View*, Fenomena Gallery, Seattle | *Choreographien*, Kunstverein Museum Schloß Moirsbroich e.V., Leverkusen **2003** *Bewegte Bilder und Fotografie*, Kunst aus NRW, Ehemalige Reichsabtei, Aachen-Kornelimünster **2002** *Bewegte Bilder*, Samuelis Baumgarte Galerie, Bielefeld **2001** *Fotografie und Video*, Dortmunder Kunstverein **1999** *Auf den Spuren des Lichts*, Palazzo Albrizzi, Venedig **1997** *Roma*, Galerie Janine Mautsch, Cologne | *Luce – Spazi*, Accademia Tedesca Villa Massimo, Rome **1995** *Fotografia*, Galleria Leonardi V-Idea, Genua | *Fotoarbeiten*, Regionalmuseum Xanten

Group Exhibitions (Selection)
2019 *1000 Wirklichkeiten – 100 Jahre GDL/DFA*, Haus der Photographie, Deichtorhallen Hamburg | *Videolounge*, imai, NRW-Forum, Düsseldorf | *Die Große Kunstausstellung NRW*, Museum Kunstpalast Düsseldorf **2018** *Architektur Plus*, Galerie Schloss Wiespach | *Landschaften*, Galerie Judith Andreae, Bonn | *Transmitter 05*, Krefelder Kunstverein | *Die Große Kunstausstellung NRW*, Museum Kunstpalast Düsseldorf **2017** *Pool*, Plan D., Die Digitale Düsseldorf | *The Planet is Blue*, Galerie Judith Andreae, Bonn | *Let's Buy It – Kunst und Einkauf*, Ludwiggalerie Schloss Oberhausen **2016** *Die Digitale Düsseldorf*, Weltkunstzimmer, Düsseldorf | *Substanzen*, Krefelder Kunstverein e.V. | *Kristalle im Beton – Die produktive Leichtigkeit*, Skulpturenmuseum Glaskasten, Marl **2014** *DEW21 Kunstpreis*, Museum für Kunst und Kulturgeschichte, Dortmund | *Mythos Wald*, Neue Galerie im Haus Beda, Bitburg **2012** *Images Against Darkness*, KIT–Kunst im Tunnel, Düsseldorf | *Bildspuren – unruhige Gegen-warten*, 7. Darmstädter Tage der Fotografie, Darmstadt | *Die Große Kunstausstellung NRW*, Museum

Kunstpalast, Düsseldorf **2011** *Windows II*, Deutscher Künstler-bund, Berlin **2010** *Spektrum der Videokunst*, Städtische Galerie, Lemgo | *Repair*, Ars Elektronica, Linz **2009** *Landscape Contemporary*, Haus der Fotografie, Burghausen | *Sample #2*, Deutscher Künstlerbund – Projektraum, Berlin | *13. Marler Video-Kunst-Preis*, ZKMax Showroom, München | *Workflow – Junge Video-Kunst in der DASA*, Dortmund **2008** *Marler Videokunstpreis*, Skulpturenmuseum Glaskasten, Marl | *European Media Art Festival*, Osnabrück | *Sample #1*, Deutscher Künstlerbund – Projektraum, Berlin **2007** *Out of Düsseldorf – German Contemporary Photography*, OMC Gallery, Huntington Beach, USA | *Fotokunst aus 60 Jahren – Kunst aus NRW unterwegs*, Galerie Münsterland e.V., Emsdetten **2006** *Straßenkunst – Meisterwerke aus drei Jahr-hunderten*, Kunsthaus Kaufbeuren | *Fotokunst aus 60 Jahren – Kunst aus NRW unterwegs*, Museum der Stadt Ratingen / Flottmannhallen Herne **2005** *architektur mobil*, Rudolf-Scharpf-Galerie, Ludwigshafen **2004** *Lichtrouten*, Lüdenscheid | *City Views*, Galerie Christa Burger, Munich | *medium medien*, Kunstverein Lingen Kunsthalle | *Let's Make Things Better*, ram foundation, Rotterdam | *Staffellauf*, Kaiser-Wilhelm-Museum, Krefeld | *Ins Licht gerückt – Werke aus der Graphischen Sammlung*, Kunstmuseum Bonn | *Von Körpern und anderen Dingen – Deutsche Fotografie von der Weimarer bis zur Berliner Republik*, Moscow House of Photography / Museum Bochum **2003** *Von Körpern und anderen Dingen – Deutsche Fotografie von der Weimarer bis zur Berliner Republik*, City Galerie Prague / Deutsches Historisches Museum Berlin |

Drehen-Kreisen-Rotieren, Kunstmuseum Ahlen **2002** *Drehen-Kreisen-Rotieren*, Museum Kulturspeicher, Würzburg / Kunstmuseum / Heidenheim / Pfalzgalerie Kaiserslautern | *heute bis jetzt*, Museum Kunstpalast, Düsseldorf | *go public – transmediale.02*, Haus der Kulturen der Welt, Berlin **2001** *Akt 1 – Die Macht der Gewohnheit*, Kunsthalle Exnergasse, Vienna | *Fotografie aus NRW*, Ehemalige Reichsabtei, Aachen / Kornelimünster | *9. Marler Videokunstpreis*, Kunstverein Hürth / Neues Museum Weserburg, Bremen / Kunsthalle Bremen / Städtische Galerie im Lenbachhaus, München / Neues Museum Weimar Kunstsammlung zu Weimar / Bellevue-Saal, Wiesbaden / Heidelberger Kunstverein **2000** *Kunst der Gegenwart aus NRW, eine Ausstellung des Landes NRW*, ZDF Sendezentrum, Mainz | *8. Marler Videokunstpreis*, Skulpturenmuseum Glaskasten Marl **1999** *8. Marler Videokunstpreis*, Blue Box-Videoforum, Bellevue-Saal, Wiesbaden / Neues Museum Weserburg, Bremen / Kunst-halle Bremen / Städtische Galerie im Lenbachhaus, Munich / Kunstverein Braunschweig / Badischer Kunstverein, Karlsruhe **1998** *Kunst und Computer*, Altonaer Museum Hamburg | *8. Marler Videokunstpreis*, Skulpturenmuseum Glaskasten Marl / Neuer Berliner Kunstverein, Berlin **1996** Bergische Kunstausstellung, Deutsches Klingenmuseum Solingen **1994** *Architektur-Fotografie*, Kulturforum Alte Post, Neuss **1992** *Architektur subjektiv*, Kunstverein Heilbronn | *Gudrun Kemsa – Marina Makowski*, Galerie Janine Mautsch, Cologne | *Bergische Kunstausstellung*, Deutsches Klingenmuseum Solingen | *Fotografie*, Kunstverein Heinsberg

**Impressum /
Colophon**

Diese Publikation erscheint anlässlich der Ausstellungen /
This book is published in conjunction with the exhibitions:

Gudrun Kemsa – NEW YORK, NEW YORK

Osthaus Museum Hagen
25.1.–1.3.2020

Museum Moderner Kunst Wörlen, Passau
6.3.–20.6.2021

Kunsthalle Erfurt
1.8.–10.10.2021

Herausgeber / Editors:
Osthaus Museum, Hagen
Museum Moderner Kunst Wörlen, Passau
Kunsthalle Erfurt

Grafische Gestaltung / Graphic Design:
Jan Buschmann, Gudrun Kemsa

Autoren / Authors:
Dr. Tayfun Belgin, Gudrun Kemsa

Lektorat / Copyediting:
Susann Harring (dt.)

Übersetzung / Translation:
Amy Klement

Herstellung / Production:
Jens Bartneck, Kerber Verlag

Projektmanagement / Project Management:
Verena Simon, Kerber Verlag

Gesamtherstellung und Vertrieb /
Printed and published by:

Kerber Verlag
Windelsbleicher Str. 166–170
33659 Bielefeld
Germany
+49 521 950 08 10
+49 521 950 08 88 (F)
info@kerberverlag.com
kerberverlag.com

KERBER Publikationen werden weltweit vertrieben /
Kerber publications are distributed worldwide:

ACC Art Books
Sandy Lane
Old Martlesham
Woodbridge, IP12 4SD
UK
+44 1394 38 99 50
+44 1394 38 99 99 (F)
accartbooks.com

Artbook | D.A.P.
75 Broad Street, Suite 630
New York, NY 10004
USA
+1 212 627 19 99
+1 212 627 94 84 (F)
artbook.com

AVA Verlagsauslieferung
Scheidegger
Obere Bahnhofstr. 10A
8910 Affoltern am Albis
Switzerland
+41 44 762 42 41
+41 44 762 42 49 (F)
avainfo@ava.ch

KNV Zeitfracht
Verlagsauslieferung
kerber-verlag@knv-zeitfracht.de

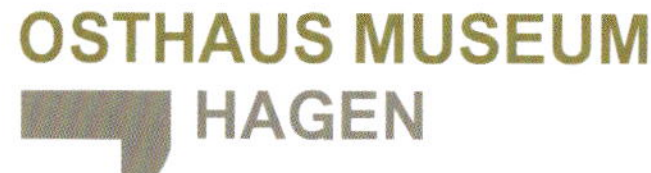
OSTHAUS MUSEUM
HAGEN

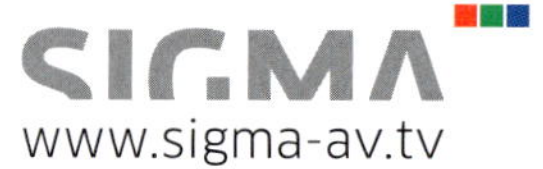
SIGMA
www.sigma-av.tv

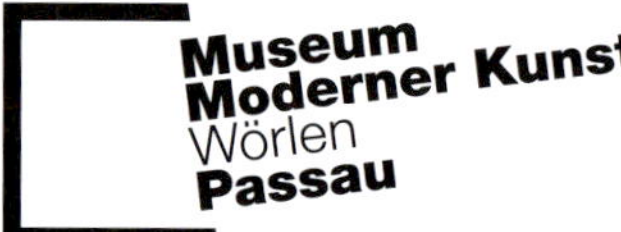
Museum
Moderner Kunst
Wörlen
Passau

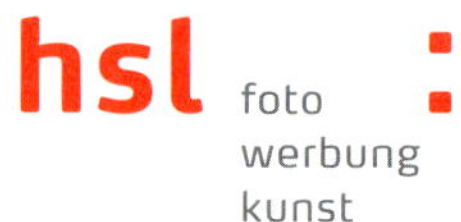
hsl
foto
werbung
kunst

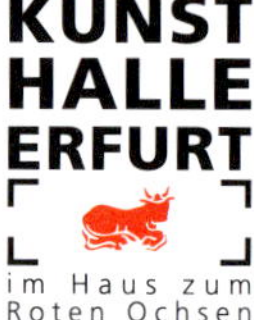
KUNST
HALLE
ERFURT
im Haus zum
Roten Ochsen

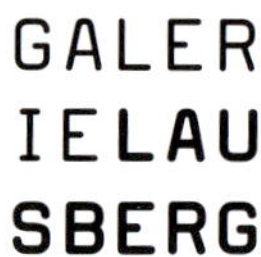
GALER
IELAU
SBERG